# One Pot

## Cookbook Vegetarian & More

Clara de Vries

151 easy vegetarian One Pot dishes quick & tasty! One Pot Vegetarian with One Pot Meals & One Pot Pasta cooking ideas for kids and family.

1st edition
2021
© All rights reserved
ISBN: 9798722175892

# Table of contents

FOREWORD .................................................................................................. 1
VEGETARIAN DIET ....................................................................................... 2
WHY ONE POT? ........................................................................................... 4
    QUICK PREPARATION IN JUST ONE POT ............................................................ 4
    ORIGIN OF THE ONE POT DISHES ...................................................................... 5
    STRUCTURE OF ONE POT RECIPES ..................................................................... 7
    COMPOSITION OF ONE POT DISHES .................................................................. 7
    RULES OF ONE POT COOKING .......................................................................... 9
EQUIPMENT .............................................................................................. 11
ADVANTAGES OF ONE POT DISHES ........................................................ 12
NOTE ON THE RECIPES ............................................................................. 14
SPREAD ..................................................................................................... 15
    *Almond Paste* ............................................................................................ 16
    *Nut Spread* ................................................................................................ 16
    *Strawberry Butter* ..................................................................................... 17
    *Jam without Sugar* ................................................................................... 17
    *Apricot Jam* .............................................................................................. 18
    *Date Cream* .............................................................................................. 18
    *Peanut Butter* ........................................................................................... 19
    *Blueberry Cream* ...................................................................................... 19
    *Herbal Pot* ................................................................................................ 20
    *Hummus with Avocado* ........................................................................... 20
    *Fruity Cream Cheese* ................................................................................ 21
    *Gouda Butter* ........................................................................................... 21
    *Coconut – Banana – Spread* ..................................................................... 22
    *Jerusalem Artichoke Tuber Spread* ......................................................... 22
BREAD ....................................................................................................... 23
    *Chia Spelt Bread* ...................................................................................... 24
    *Farmhouse Bread* .................................................................................... 25
BREAKFAST ............................................................................................... 26
    *Cinnamon Crunchy Flakes* ....................................................................... 27
    *Vegan Porridge with Vanilla* .................................................................... 27
    *Fig and Mulberry Porridge with Almonds* .............................................. 28
    *Fruity Couscous* ....................................................................................... 29
    *Vegan Chocolate Porridge* ....................................................................... 29
    *Blueberry Quinoa Porridge* ...................................................................... 30

- *Oriental Rice Pudding* ............................................................................................. 31
- *Delicious Birch Muesli* ............................................................................................. 32
- *Vegan Strawberry Banana Smoothie* ..................................................................... 33
- *Raspberry Smoothie* ............................................................................................... 33
- *Quinoa Breakfast Porridge* ..................................................................................... 34
- *Quick Semolina Porridge* ........................................................................................ 34
- *Breakfast Smoothie* ................................................................................................ 35
- *Vegan Pick-Me-Up Smoothie* ................................................................................. 35
- *Good Morning Soup* ............................................................................................... 36
- *Crunchy Granola* .................................................................................................... 37
- *Mango Breakfast Lassi* ........................................................................................... 38
- *Green Power Smoothie* .......................................................................................... 38
- *Exotic Smoothie* ...................................................................................................... 39
- *Red Good Mood Smoothie* .................................................................................... 39

## ONE POT PASTA ...........................................................................................................40

- *One Pot Pasta Viva Italia* ........................................................................................ 41
- *Spring One Pot* ....................................................................................................... 42
- *Coconut One Pot Curry* .......................................................................................... 43
- *One Pot Pasta alla Napoletana* .............................................................................. 44
- *One Pot Pasta al Funghi* ......................................................................................... 45
- *Spaetzle Vegetable One Pot* .................................................................................. 45
- *Thai One Pot Pasta* ................................................................................................. 46
- *One Pot Vegetable Soup with Pasta* ...................................................................... 47
- *Colourful Pasta One Pot* ........................................................................................ 48
- *One-Pot Tomato Pasta* ........................................................................................... 49
- *Alloy One Pot Noodle Soup* ................................................................................... 50
- *Tomato Spinach One Pot Pasta* .............................................................................. 51
- *Autumn Pumpkin One Pot* ..................................................................................... 52
- *Courgette Tomato One Pot* ................................................................................... 53
- *Mac 'n' Cheese One Pot* ......................................................................................... 54
- *Spinach Tomato One Pot Pasta* .............................................................................. 55
- *Mushroom One Pot Pasta with Gorgonzola* .......................................................... 56
- *One Pot Pasta alla Caprese* .................................................................................... 57
- *One Pot Pasta alla Genovese* ................................................................................. 58
- *Pasta-Vegetable-One-Pot* ...................................................................................... 59
- *Fried Thai Noodles One Pot* ................................................................................... 60
- *Broccoli One Pot Pasta* ........................................................................................... 60
- *Exotic Coconut Tomato One Pot Pasta* .................................................................. 61
- *Peanut Ginger One Pot Pasta* ................................................................................ 62

## ONE POT MAIN DISHES..............................................................................................63

- *Quinoa Vegetable One Pot* .................................................................................... 64
- *Pumpkin Lentil Chili sin Carne* ............................................................................... 65
- *Oriental Rice One Pot* ............................................................................................ 66

| | |
|---|---|
| Greek Style Rice One Pot | 67 |
| Indian Lentil Dhal One Pot | 68 |
| Potato Spinach One Pot Curry | 69 |
| Low Carb One Pot | 70 |
| Chana Masala One Pot | 71 |
| Oriental Lentil Rice One Pot | 72 |
| Risotto with Lemon and Celery | 73 |
| Simple Vegetable Rice | 74 |
| Rice One Pot alla Genovese | 74 |
| One-Pot Risotto | 75 |
| Pumpkin Polenta One Pot | 75 |
| One-Pot Ratatouille | 76 |
| Vegetable Egg One Pot | 76 |
| Potato-Broccoli-One-Pot | 77 |
| Carrot and Potato Puree | 77 |
| Delicious Vegetable Cream One Pot | 78 |
| One Pot Gnocchi in Tomato Sauce | 78 |
| Thai Curry One Pot Gnocchi | 79 |
| Gnocchi One Pot Caprese | 79 |
| One Pot Curry with Cauliflower | 80 |
| Leek and Potato One-Pot | 80 |
| Veggie Yakisoba One Pot | 81 |
| One-Pot Vegetable Spaetzle | 81 |
| Courgette Noodles Alla Carbonara | 82 |
| Mediterranean Style Quinoa Salad | 83 |
| Exotic One Pot Coconut Lentil Curry | 84 |
| Oriental Millet One Pot | 85 |
| Millet-Amaranth-One-Pot | 86 |
| One Pot Rice with Vegetables | 87 |
| Quinoa Tofu One Pot | 88 |
| Potato Salad One Pot | 89 |
| Asian Rice Noodle One Pot | 89 |
| Vegan Carrot One Pot Risotto | 90 |
| Vegan Bulgur Salad | 91 |
| Vegan Rice Pudding | 91 |
| Vegan Lentil Bolognese One Pot for Kids | 92 |
| Colourful Salad | 92 |
| Tofu Vegetable One Pot | 93 |
| Chili-sin-Carne-con-Soja | 94 |
| Vegan Vegetable Curry | 95 |
| Moroccan Quinoa One Pot | 96 |
| One-Pot Quinoa Bowl | 97 |
| **SNACKS** | **98** |
| Sheet Pan Kale Chips | 99 |

*Fresh Goat Cheese and Melon Salad* .................................................................. *99*
*Vanilla Cinnamon Almond Snack* ..................................................................... *100*
*Chips Low Carb* ................................................................................................ *100*
*Cheese Balls* ..................................................................................................... *101*
*Hummus with Vegetable Sticks* ...................................................................... *101*
*Sesame Sunflower Crackers* ........................................................................... *102*

**DESSERT** .................................................................................................................**103**
*Coconut Semolina Porridge* ............................................................................ *104*
*Chocolate Nut Cookie One Pot* ....................................................................... *104*
*After-Eight Chocolate Cream* .......................................................................... *105*
*Berry Semolina Porridge* ................................................................................. *105*
*Banana Chia Pudding* ...................................................................................... *106*
*Vanilla Pudding with Chocolate Sauce* ........................................................... *106*
*Crispy Low Carb Cinnamon Wafers* ................................................................ *107*
*Express Dessert Chocolate Banana* ................................................................ *107*
*Vegan Raw Food Dessert* ................................................................................ *108*
*Colourful Fruit Island* ...................................................................................... *108*
*Greek Style Yoghurt* ........................................................................................ *109*
*Vegan Chocolate Porridge* .............................................................................. *109*
*Waffles with Coconut* ..................................................................................... *110*
*Fruit Bar* .......................................................................................................... *110*
*Apple Pancakes with Wholemeal Flour* ......................................................... *111*

**ICE CREAM** ............................................................................................................**112**
*Banana Ice Cream* ........................................................................................... *113*
*Melon Ice Cream* ............................................................................................. *113*
*Avocado Ice Cream* ......................................................................................... *114*
*Mango-Pineapple-Coconut Ice Cream* ........................................................... *115*
*Raspberry Banana Ice Cream* ......................................................................... *115*
*Strawberry Yoghurt Ice Cream* ....................................................................... *116*
*Fruit Lollipop* ................................................................................................... *116*
*Apricot and Coconut Ice Cream* ..................................................................... *117*
*Berry Ice Cream* .............................................................................................. *117*
*Raspberry-Mango Ice Cream* .......................................................................... *118*
*Yoghurt Ice Cream Vanilla Mango* .................................................................. *118*
*Strawberry Ice Cream* ..................................................................................... *119*
*Frozen Yoghurt* ................................................................................................ *119*
*Kiwi Popsicle* .................................................................................................... *120*
*Capri Ice Cream a la Casa* ............................................................................... *120*

**DRINKS** ..................................................................................................................**121**
*Herbal Ginger Spice Tea* ................................................................................. *122*
*Infused Water* .................................................................................................. *122*
*Pineapple-Lime Drink* ..................................................................................... *123*

*Lemon Ginger Lemonade* ............................................................................... *123*
*Peach Iced Tea* ............................................................................................... *124*
*Pomegranate Lemonade* ............................................................................... *124*
*Cucumber Mint Lemonade* ............................................................................ *125*
*Strawberry and Rosehip Iced Tea* ................................................................. *125*
*Orange-Lemon Iced Tea* ................................................................................ *126*

**CLOSING WORDS** .............................................................................................**127**

# Foreword

Do you like to cook, but sometimes just don't have the time for elaborate dishes? Is a healthy balanced diet important to you, but usually not worth the effort? Do you value a varied and diverse diet, but don't want to spend a lot of work and time in the kitchen?

Then you've come to the right place with this book, because it shows you a variety of healthy, balanced and varied dishes that you can easily prepare in "one pot".

When compiling the recipes, I have paid great attention to a diverse selection of vegetarian products. This way you can prepare delicious, nutritious and quick meals. That's why one-pot recipes are particularly suitable for stressful working days or for days when you simply don't feel like cooking for a long time.

Put an end to fast food as a stopgap, and try the one-pot recipes instead! This way you can please yourself or your whole family with a delicious dish without having to spend hours cooking and cleaning up. Why not try it out, discover new recipes or get to know your favourite dishes in a new way!

# Vegetarian diet

A vegetarian diet has long ceased to have anything to do with renunciation or pure raw food. In the meantime, vegetarian cuisine has become a kind of modern and popular nutrition trend that promises healthy, balanced, tasty and filling meals. Because vegetarian dishes are available today in all variations, with surprising combinations or exciting spice creations, so that the vegetarian diet is not inferior to omnivorous cuisine in terms of culinary variety or taste. This is not surprising, as the renunciation of meat is known in all nations and is even preferred in some cultural circles, such as India. Therefore, it is considered outdated to associate vegetarian nutrition with boredom, monotony or lack. Instead, there are no limits to vegetarian cuisine, and a wide variety of dishes can be prepared in all directions of taste and enjoyment.

This is because there is a wide range of vegetarian products that can be used and combined. For example, a vegetarian meal does not mean the limited consumption of vegetables or salad, but cereal products, potatoes, pulses, vegetables, fruit, sauces, spices, and depending on the diet, even cheese, cream and eggs can be used. In addition, vegetarian substitutes made from tofu or soy are now available in many supermarkets, so that vegetarians no longer necessarily have to do without delicious dishes with soy-based minced meat, tofu nuggets or soy cutlets.

The overall result is that a comprehensive and sufficient supply of nutrients and coverage of all vital substances, vitamins, proteins and other minerals can be achieved through a vegetarian diet. Even the supply of essential nutrients often referred to as deficiencies, such as iron, vitamin B12, vitamin D, iodine or proteins, can be ensured by a sufficient, diverse, healthy and varied diet with purely vegetarian products.

Furthermore, abstaining from meat can even have positive effects on health. Scientific studies have already shown that a vegetarian diet can lower cholesterol levels, influence blood sugar levels and regulate blood pressure. This has positive effectss on the body, so that the risk of developing arteriosclerosis, diabetes, bowel cancer or cardiovascular problems or suffering a stroke or heart attack can be reduced.

Therefore, it is quite understandable if you have decided to go vegetarian for health reasons or for moral or ethical reasons. Because apart from factory farming, the excessive use of antibiotics or the impactful damage to the environment, there are many other reasons that can speak in favour of giving up meat. For this reason, this book gives you the opportunity to get to know your vegetarian diet in a completely new way by trying out a different way of cooking. For this purpose, the "One Pot Recipes" offer you a variety of suggestions on how to prepare vegetarian dishes in a simple, quick and yet healthy and varied way. You may even discover completely new vegetarian dishes!

# Why One Pot?

You've probably heard of "one pot meals" before, because this type of cooking is considered a modern cooking trend. And with good reason, because the recipes are not only quick and easy, but also really delicious!

The popularity and familiarity of this food trend is not surprising, however, when you consider its origins. Strictly speaking, "one-pot meals" are not a newfangled trend, but the revival of one of the oldest and most widespread cooking methods. Since it has always been suitable for preparing delicious and substantial meals with little effort, even for many guests, one can understand why it has long proven itself in many kitchens. But how do "one pot recipes" work?

## Quick Preparation in Just One Pot

The term "one pot" comes from English and means nothing other than "one pot". So, this type of dish has existed in Germany for a long time, because even our grandmothers prepared nutritious, hearty stews. Overall, "one pot dishes" can also be compared to the classic stew. This is because both variants involve cooking a base of cereal products or pulses with liquids, spices and vegetables in a pot to create a delicious meal.

Nevertheless, there are significant differences between the two dishes: The main purpose of a stew is to warm and fill you up. It usually consists of potatoes, cereals or pulses with vegetables or meat and is characterised by the fact that it has to cook for a long time. The end product is a wholesome soup. The variety of "one pot dishes", on the other hand, knows no bounds: Everything is possible via soups, salads, pasta, rice or potatoes! The aim is not just to fill you up, but the recipes place great emphasis on a simple, yet healthy and balanced diet.

# Origin of the One Pot Dishes

The origin of the "stew" probably lies in Northern Germany or East Prussia, as people there cooked over an open fire for a long time and did not have a variable cooking area or a closed cooker. This made it practical and necessary to cook different ingredients together in one cauldron. In addition, the stew played an important role in the First World War, as large masses of soldiers had to be fed at that time. For a stew you could prepare large quantities and many different foods at the same time and thus feed many people.

However, this use of stews to feed the war soldiers led to the stew being considered a poor man's or peasant's dish for a long time. Later, under National Socialism, the stew became a symbol of community, equal and shared food, which was supposed to place national commonality above social differences.

This way of cooking together and then eating a nutritious and varied meal together from just one pot is probably thousands of years old. It is assumed that this cooking technique was known or is known in almost all cultural circles. Examples of this are the Roman cereal porridge, which contained pulses (e.g. beans) in addition to various grains such as barley. Or the North American hominy, which consisted of maize, beans and fish or meat. But even today, many cultures have stews, such as the Indian curry or the Japanese nabemono.

Nevertheless, "one pot meals" are considered a modern food trend, which probably first became known through the American TV chef Martha Stewart. The US-American comes from New Jersey and works as an author, presenter, entrepreneur and cook. Her goal is to make everyday life and household chores easier and less stressful, but without sacrificing sophistication and style. To this end, she is always spreading great recipes or easy tips and tricks that significantly improve the household with little effort.

For this reason, she is considered the "best housewife" in the USA, from whom one can learn a lot.

In this context, Martha Stewart was the first cook to spread recipes for the modern one-pot pasta. She used a tomato sauce with basil and pasta and cooked everything together in one pot. All in all, for a "One Pot Pasta" you prepare the sauce and the vegetables as well as the pasta in one pot. However, since there are endless variations of pasta dishes, it is not surprising that this idea was quickly spread and varied. Moreover, this idea was developed further and further, so that today there are no longer only recipes for "one pot pasta", but actually a wide variety and combination possibilities of different "one pot dishes".

This means that "One Pot Recipes" are not only instructions for nutritious soup or stews, but they offer a wide variation of ingredients, combinations and dishes, so that there are hardly any limits to the trend. That's why cooking according to "One Pot Recipes" is not only suitable for people who don't feel like or don't have time to cook, but for anyone who wants to try out new things or prepare varied dishes. This way you can inspire yourself, your whole family or your friends with a great meal!

# Structure of One Pot Recipes

Basically, every "One Pot recipe" works the same way: the idea is to put different ingredients in a pot one after the other and cook them together to get a varied meal. Nevertheless, there are a few rules to follow, as not every dish can be converted into an "on pot dish". In addition, the choice of ingredients must also be taken into account, as some things are better suited than others. For this reason, the most important rules for ingredient selection, composition and preparation of "One Pot dishes" are described and explained below. In addition, these rules, quantities and procedures are automatically implemented in our recipes, so that you can simply follow the instructions and procedures of the recipes to obtain delicious dishes from just one pot!

# Composition of One Pot Dishes

A vegetarian "one pot meal" always consists of at least three ingredients: First, you need a base, which is the main ingredient of the meal. This is then supplemented with different vegetables. Finally, you need certain liquids that you can refine by adding herbs or spices. This means that "one pot recipes" also follow a specific structure. Therefore, it is important to select suitable foods to achieve the desired result.

Carbohydrate foods such as potatoes, rice, quinoa, millet, bulgur, couscous or pasta are particularly suitable as a basis for "one pot dishes". Alternatively, pulses are also a suitable basis. These include lentils, chickpeas and various beans. Tofu, which is made from soybeans, can also serve as a base.

The second important component for vegetarian "one pot dishes" is the vegetables. There are no limits to the selection and variation, so that new and exciting "one pot dishes" can always be created. However, there are some types of vegetables that are better suited for preparation in a pot than others. This is because a short cooking time and a high variety of flavour combinations are particularly advantageous. For this reason, vegetables such as tomatoes, spinach, corn, mushrooms, broccoli, cauliflower, peppers, aubergine and courgettes are particularly suitable for use in "one pot recipes". Onions, garlic or ginger can also be used as flavour carriers. The advantage of these vegetables is that they can be combined with various spices, liquids and bases to create delicious dishes and they only need a short time to become soft.

Finally, the choice of liquids, herbs and spices is decisive for the taste of the finished "One Pot dish". Depending on the selection, you can give the meal a Mediterranean, Asian, Latin American or various other flavour. This means that you can always try out new variants and variations and prepare varied dishes.

Therefore, you first choose a liquid in which to cook the base. This liquid also forms the basis for the sauce of the dish. You can simply and classically use water, but cream, bouillon, wine, strained tomatoes or coconut milk are also excellent for "one pot dishes", so you can use them flexibly according to your preferences and wishes. Then you should choose suitable spices and herbs to round off your meal and give it a special flavour. Salt and pepper can always form the basis to achieve a general seasoning. In addition, you can add curry, paprika, oregano, herbs de Provence or many more to your dish. Alternatively, you can use fresh herbs such as basil, chives, parsley, rosemary or coriander and use them as you like. But tomato paste, cream cheese, feta, curry paste or soy sauce are also great for rounding off your "one pot dishes". As you can see, there are no limits to your creativity in "One Pot cooking"!

Since the selection and combination possibilities of "one pot dishes" are diverse and seemingly endless, we have compiled various recipes in this cookbook that will present you with a delicious result. This way, you can rely on our pre-selection and enjoy great recipes directly, without having to try out, modify and improve different variations beforehand. This cookbook therefore makes it easier for you to get started with "One Pot Cooking", but you can also take it to hand again and again to conjure up great dishes that you can rely on to be successful with little effort!

## Rules of One Pot Cooking

Although "one pot recipes" are by and large clearly structured and easy and quick to implement, there are still a few basic rules that you should follow when cooking this way. Because there are some general procedures that are necessary for you to succeed with the "one pot dishes". For this, it is necessary that all the ingredients are added to the pot in the right order and that they are cooked for a sufficient time so that they are done. Therefore, the following rules can help you when cooking "one pot recipes":

- **These special features apply when cooking in a saucepan:**

  - Unlike large, flat pans, in which the heat is distributed evenly over the entire vessel, saucepans are cut rather high and have only a small contact surface on the cooker in proportion. This means that the heat is much higher at the bottom of the pot than further up. For this reason, you should put the basic ingredients, such as rice, pasta or potatoes, into the pot first, so that they get enough heat and become cooked.

  - Moreover, when cooking in a pot, it is necessary to stir again and again. Otherwise there is a risk that the lower ingredients will burn or stick to the bottom of the pot, even though the upper ingredients are not yet cooked soft.

- **This is what you should consider with the liquids:**

- Although cream, coconut milk or strained tomatoes are suitable liquids for preparing "one pot dishes", you should always add some water. This is because the basic ingredients need a lot of liquid to cook. Therefore, although you should use water sparingly to achieve a creamy sauce, you should always monitor the liquid intake to ensure that all ingredients are cooked sufficiently.

- Using the right amount of liquid to achieve cooked ingredients but still creamy and non-watery sauces is a balancing act. That's why we always give you the right ratio of the different liquids in the recipes, so that your "One Pot dishes" are a great success.

- **These are the rules you should follow when preparing vegetables:**

    - One Pot meals are designed to be an easy and quick alternative for you to prepare healthy meals with little effort. That's why our recipes are specially designed so that they require little work and cooking time. However, it is necessary that you cut the vegetables as small as possible. This way you can effectively reduce the cooking time and quickly achieve a delicious result.

    - Conversely, it is also important that the vegetables in your pot do not cook too long, as they will otherwise become too soft and lose their taste and consistency. For this reason, you should add the vegetables to the pot first, when the basic ingredient has already cooked a little. You should also follow an order to add the vegetable with the shortest cooking time last. This rule is also included in our recipes, so you can easily follow the descriptions and instructions.

# Equipment

In addition to observing these rules, the right choice of equipment is also crucial for the success of "one pot meals". Therefore, the most important basics for preparing delicious meals in one pot are described here:

Overall, the special feature of "one pot recipes" is that they can be prepared in only one cooking pot. This is why the pot is the most important and decisive basis for a successful realisation of the dishes. For this reason, when choosing a pot, you should make sure that it is big enough to cook all the ingredients together. There is nothing more annoying than cooking in a pot that is too small and cannot be stirred without some of the ingredients ending up next to the pot. So, don't underestimate the size you need and go for a pot that is too big rather than too small.

In addition, you need nothing more than a chopping board, a kitchen knife and a wooden spoon to prepare "one pot dishes". You need these things to chop the vegetables and stir the ingredients in the pot. It is also useful to use a measuring cup to add the right amount of liquid.

Apart from that, you don't need any other equipment to cook delicious "one pot recipes". That's why preparation is quick and easy and the amount of washing up afterwards is very limited.

# Advantages of One Pot Dishes

In everyday life, it is often difficult to have enough time for a balanced, nutritious diet in addition to work, household chores, leisure activities, voluntary work and many other aspects. Besides, no one wants to spend hours in the kitchen after a hard day.

This is the biggest advantage of the "One Pot Recipes": They show you how you can cook delicious, healthy and varied meals with little effort. This means you can prepare nutritious meals even during stressful periods. But not only do you save time when cooking, but also cleaning up is really quick: because you only use one pot to prepare all the ingredients! This eliminates the need to wash various pots, pans and bowls and instead you can cook and serve everything in one pot and only have to clean up this one pot.

In addition, "one pot recipes" are also particularly well suited to everyday family life. This is because children often have different preferences than adults, so some parents cook several dishes at the same time to cater to all tastes. However, popular children's dishes usually consist of a base with sauce or vegetables, such as pasta with tomato sauce, and can therefore be prepared super as a "one pot dish". This saves you extra stress and effort.

But even if you basically have the time to cook, for example because you have invited visitors, one-pot recipes can be an advantage. They allow you to have less stress before your guests arrive, because you don't have to frantically use everything your kitchen has to offer. Instead, you gradually add all the ingredients to the pot and let it simmer slowly. This way you can greet your guests relaxed and with a clean kitchen! This way, you can concentrate on your guests and the conversations during the evening and stay as long as you like. Because I don't expect a messy kitchen afterwards that you have to tediously clean up late at night or the next morning.

In addition, "one pot recipes" are also suitable for people who don't like to cook or don't cook often. Because the parallel preparation, cooking and seasoning of rice or pasta, sauce and vegetables can quickly lead to losing track or feeling stressed. However, if you decide on a "one pot meal", this can't happen to you. Because you have enough time to prepare the ingredients step by step and put them in the pot one after the other, so you can relax and concentrate on just one thing and don't have to monitor and carry out several processes at the same time. The annoying running back and forth in the kitchen is no longer necessary and the probability of burning part of the food due to carelessness is also very low. Cooking is therefore much less complicated and more pleasant.

The preparation of "one pot meals" has a multitude of advantages for you! Whether you choose to cook this way to save time, to lighten the load of your daily routine, to try new things or to integrate delicious alternatives into your eating habits, "one pot recipes" are suitable for many occasions.

So please yourself, your family or your friends with delicious, varied and diverse "one pot meals" and save yourself the stress of cooking and the work of cleaning up afterwards!

# Note on the recipes

Before we start with the recipes, I would like to give you a few important tips on the structure of the recipes. As this is not my first cookbook, I already have good experience of what readers expect from a cookbook.

**Why does this cookbook not contain any photos of the dishes?**

Some readers wonder about the lack of illustrations of recipes in cookbooks, e.g. on Amazon. To forestall the wonderment, here is an explanation from me:

Cooking and guidebooks are my passion. In order to share my passion with as many people as possible, I try to offer my books at an affordable price. However, this concern is not feasible with colour photos in books, as the printing costs are doubled. If you add the shipping costs, this leads to an enormous increase in costs.

Especially in this book, the added value of illustrations seems to me to be very limited.

If you have ever cooked a dish from a cookbook, you have certainly noticed that your dish usually looks different from the picture in the cookbook. This is because the pictures are also intended more as illustrations.

Putting over 150 pictures in a cookbook is in my opinion, not helpful and doesn't fill you up. I have therefore aimed for a variety of one-pot dishes to give you as much variety as possible.

As a bonus, there are also refreshing ice cream recipes and delicious lemonades!

# ONE POT
## VEGETARIAN & MORE

## SPREAD

15

# Almond Paste

### Ingredients:

- 500 grams unpeeled almonds
- a pinch of cinnamon

### Preparation:

1. First, preheat the oven to 150 degrees and then roast the almonds on a baking tray for about 5 minutes - then the almonds should cool down a bit.
2. Take a blender and puree the almonds on the lowest setting. Then add the cinnamon. Pause for a moment and blend again for about 1 ½ minutes, but now on a higher setting. Repeat the process until you have a creamy almond paste.

# Nut Spread

### Ingredients:

- 200 grams cashew nuts
- 1 tbsp. oil
- 1 tsp lemon juice
- 100 grams apple syrup

### Preparation:

1. Puree all the ingredients in a food processor or with a hand blender to a homogeneous mixture.
2. Fill the finished nut spread into preserving jars and the delicious spread is ready!

## Strawberry Butter

### Ingredients:

- 250 grams strawberries
- three sprigs of mint
- 250 grams butter

### Preparation:

1. After washing the strawberries, remove the stem end and cut them into slices.
2. Now heat the strawberries in a saucepan over low heat until a thick mixture is formed - you should stir constantly while heating. Then stir in the finely chopped mint. Then let the mixture cool down a little.
3. Finally, stir the butter until fluffy and mix with the strawberry mixture - the delicious strawberry butter is ready.

## Jam without Sugar

### Ingredients:

- 300 grams of any fruit
- a sachet of agar- agar
- 150 ml apple juice

### Preparation:

1. Puree the peeled and seeded fruit of your choice and then gradually add the apple juice and agar-agar - then mix everything together well.
2. Now put everything together in a pot and boil it down to a thick mixture.
3. Then fill the finished jam into jars. Turn the jars upside down for about 3 minutes, then turn them over and let them cool. Closed, the jam will keep for up to four weeks - opened, however, it will only keep for seven days in the fridge.

# Apricot Jam

### Ingredients:

- 250 grams soft apricots
- 70 ml orange juice without added sugar
- 30 ml water

### Preparation:

1. Puree all ingredients finely with a blender or hand blender.
2. Now fill the mixture into a preserving jar and store it in the refrigerator. It is best to use the jam within a week.

# Date Cream

### Ingredients:

- 100 grams ground hazelnuts
- 80 ml water
- 75 grams unsulphured dates
- 1- 2 tbsp. carob
- Vanilla to taste
- 2 tablespoons coconut oil

### Preparation:

1. Soak the dates overnight.
2. Put all the ingredients in a tall container and mix everything well with a hand blender. Mix until you get a creamy mixture. If the cream is too dry, you can also add a little water.
3. The spread will keep refrigerated for up to two weeks.

# Peanut Butter

### Ingredients:

- 1 tbsp agave syrup
- 2 tablespoons peanut oil
- 220 grams peanuts

### Preparation:

1. Roast the peanuts in a pan without oil. Then let them cool down a little.
2. Chop the nuts, oil and agave syrup in a food processor or with a hand blender. Then fill the finished puree into a jar and leave the mixture to chill in the fridge.

# Blueberry Cream

### Ingredients:
### (For four servings)

- 80 grams butter
- One lemon
- 250 grams blueberries
- 1 tablespoon pear syrup

### Preparation:

1. First, wash and clean the blueberries.
2. Then grate the lemon peel and squeeze the lemon.
3. Put the berries, the juice of the lemon and the pear syrup in a pot and boil everything. Then add the butter and stir.
4. Now, mix in the lemon zest and chill the delicious spread.

# Herbal Pot

### Ingredients:
(For four servings)

- A bunch of chives
- A bunch of parsley
- A bunch of dill
- 500 grams low-fat quark
- 150 ml milk

### Preparation:

1. Chop the herbs finely.
2. Then mix the curd with the milk and add the herbs.

## Hummus with Avocado

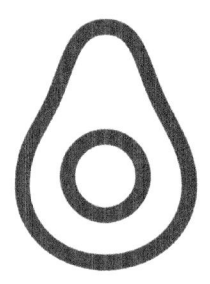

### Ingredients:
(For approx. 150 grams of hummus)

- 300 grams cooked chickpeas incl. broth
- 2 tbsp. lemon juice
- 3 tbsp olive oil
- One very ripe avocado
- ½ tsp ground coriander

### Preparation:

1. First, cook the chickpeas, pass them through a sieve and collect the broth - keep it.
2. Then puree the chickpeas with the lemon juice, olive oil, ground coriander and 3 tablespoons of stock.
3. Then add the avocado flesh and puree it as well. Then add the chickpea broth until the perfect hummus consistency is achieved.

# Fruity Cream Cheese

## Ingredients:

- Fresh fruit (e.g. pear, berries, banana)
- 100 grams pure cream cheese

## Preparation:

1. Put the cream cheese and fruit of your choice in a bowl or blender and blend until it is creamy. The fruity cream cheese can be kept in the fridge for about 3 days.

# Gouda Butter

## Ingredients:
### (For four servings)

- 250 grams butter
- 100 grams Gouda

## Preparation:

1. Beat the butter until fluffy. Then grate the Gouda cheese finely and stir in the butter. The spread is ready!

# Coconut – Banana – Spread

## Ingredients:
(For six servings)

- 150 grams grated coconut
- 40 grams coconut oil
- Three ripe bananas
- 1 tablespoon lemon juice
- A pinch of ground cinnamon

## Preparation:

1. Peel the bananas and roughly chop them. Then mash the bananas to a pulp with a fork.
2. Heat the coconut oil over medium heat and stir it into the banana mash.
3. Now add the rest of the ingredients to the mashed bananas - you should stir until you get a creamy mixture.

# Jerusalem Artichoke Tuber Spread

## Ingredients:
(For two servings)

- 4 tbsp. sunflower oil
- 5 tbsp (homemade) almond paste
- 1 ½ tbsp Jerusalem artichoke powder
- Vanilla powder to taste
- 1 ½ tbsp. carob powder

## Preparation:

1. Stir the almond paste and oil in a bowl until smooth. Then add the Jerusalem artichoke and carob and mix everything together.
2. If you like, you can add some vanilla powder and season the spread accordingly.

# ONE POT
## VEGETARIAN & MORE

## BREAD

# Chia Spelt Bread

### Ingredients for 1 loaf:

- 500 g wholemeal spelt flour
- 130 g sunflower seeds
- 20 g chia seeds
- Salt
- 1 sachet dry yeast
- 2 tablespoons apple cider vinegar
- 500 ml water

*Also:*
Box baking tin (28 cm long) or similar

### Preparation:

1. Mix all the dry ingredients together in a bowl.
2. Add the water and apple vinegar and mix with a hand mixer (dough hook) until a smooth dough form.
3. Line or grease a loaf tin with baking paper and sprinkle with flour. Spread the dough evenly in the tin. Place the loaf tin in a cold oven on the middle shelf. Now heat the oven to 200 degrees top and bottom heat and bake the bread for 1 hour. Then remove the bread from the oven. After cooling, turn the bread out of the loaf tin.

*Tip:*
If you like it spicier, you can stir 1-2 teaspoons of bread spice into the dough.

# Farmhouse Bread

## Ingredients for 1 loaf:

- 10 g organic fresh baker's yeast
- 300 g organic wholemeal wheat flour
- 150 g organic wheat flour
- 60 g organic spelt flour
- 50 g wholemeal rye sourdough, dry
- 10 g salt

*Also:*
Cast iron pot with lid

## Preparation:

1. Dissolve the yeast in 400 ml lukewarm water. Knead the different types of flour, wholemeal rye sourdough powder and the water-yeast mixture with the dough hook of a hand mixer for 5 minutes. Let the dough rest for 20 minutes.
2. Add the salt and knead the dough for another 5 minutes until it comes away easily from the edge of the bowl. Leave to rise for 1 hour. Fold to the centre with a dough scraper every 15 minutes. This will trap extra air in the dough.
3. Line a large bowl with a towel and flour it really well. Turn the dough out onto a floured work surface. With slightly moistened hands, fold all four sides from the outside in. Place in the lined bowl with the resulting seal seam facing upwards and leave covered to rise for 30 minutes. Meanwhile, preheat the pan in the oven to the highest setting (250 degrees top/- and bottom heat).
4. Remove the pan from the oven. Turn the dough out of the bowl into the pot. Hold the cloth while doing this. Put the lid on and bake in the oven. The bread is ready when it sounds hollow when tapped.

# ONE POT
## VEGETARIAN & MORE

## BREAKFAST

26

# Cinnamon Crunchy Flakes

**Ingredients for 2 servings:**
**Preparation time: approx. 5 minutes**

- 250 ml milk or vegetable milk
- 1 tablespoon cinnamon, ground
- 2 tablespoons maple syrup
- 8 crispy breads e.g. Leicht & Cross or Filinchen

### Preparation:

1. First, chop the crispbread into coarse pieces.
2. Mix the maple syrup and cinnamon in a bowl and fold in the crunchy bits.
3. Prepare two bowls of milk and divide the crispy flakes evenly.
4. Serve with fresh fruit if desired.

# Vegan Porridge with Vanilla

**Ingredients for 4 servings:**
**Preparation time: approx. 15 minutes**

- 200 g tender oat flakes
- 1 tablespoon bourbon vanilla, ground
- 1 pinch cinnamon, ground
- 2 tablespoons maple syrup
- 850 ml rice or oat milk
- Topping: e.g. strawberries, bananas, blueberries, apples, nuts, chia seeds

### Preparation:

1. Put the oat flakes, cinnamon, vanilla and maple syrup in a pot with the milk. Boil and remove from the heat. Cover and leave to soak for about 10 minutes.
2. In the meantime, you can prepare the topping. Cut the fruit of your choice into bite-sized pieces.
3. Divide the finished porridge into four portions, garnish with the topping and serve immediately.

# Fig and Mulberry Porridge with Almonds

## Ingredients for 2 servings:
## Preparation time: approx. 15 minutes

- 140 grams tender oat flakes
- 4 figs
- 16 Mulberries
- 1 teaspoon bourbon vanilla, ground
- 1 teaspoon cardamom, ground
- 1 tablespoon cinnamon, ground
- 2 tablespoons maple syrup
- 400 ml almond milk
- Topping: 2 tablespoons almond puree, 2 tablespoons almonds, chopped

## Preparation:

1. Cut the figs into small pieces and halve the mulberries.
2. Put the oat flakes, figs and mulberries in a saucepan, bring to the boil briefly. Remove from the heat, cover and let it swell for about 10 minutes.
3. Now stir in the cardamom, cinnamon and vanilla and divide into two portions.
4. Garnish the finished porridge with the almond paste and almonds and serve immediately.

# Fruity Couscous

**Ingredients for 2 servings:**
Preparation time: approx. 15 minutes

- 60 grams couscous
- 1 Orange
- 1 pear
- 2 tablespoons sultanas
- 1 pinch cinnamon, ground
- 125 ml orange juice

## Preparation:

1. First, mix the couscous with the sultanas, cinnamon and orange juice in a bowl. Let everything soak for about 10-15 minutes.
2. Peel the orange and cut it into thin slices, also slice the pear.
3. Before serving, garnish your fruity couscous with the orange and pear slices.

# Vegan Chocolate Porridge

**Ingredients for 2 servings:**
Preparation time: approx. 15 minutes

- 90 grams tender oat flakes
- 1 pinch cinnamon, ground
- 1 tablespoon cocoa powder
- 1 tablespoon maple syrup
- 300 ml hazelnut milk or almond milk

Topping: 1 banana, 1 tablespoon nuts, chopped

## Preparation:

1. Put the oat flakes with the cocoa, cinnamon, maple syrup and milk in a saucepan and bring to the boil. Remove from the heat and cover and leave to soak for about 10 minutes.
2. For the topping, slice the banana.
3. Before serving, divide the porridge into two portions and garnish with the banana slices and chopped nuts.

# Blueberry Quinoa Porridge

**Ingredients for 4 servings:**
**Preparation time: approx. 15 minutes**

- 400 grams quinoa
- 1 pinch cinnamon, ground
- 1 pulp of a vanilla pod
- 1 tablespoon honey or agave syrup
- 500 ml milk
- Topping: 150 g blueberries, 25 g almond leaves

**Preparation:**

1. Prepare the quinoa according to the instructions on the packet.
2. Mix the milk with the cinnamon and vanilla pulp.
3. Before serving, divide the quinoa into four portions, pour over the milk, drizzle with honey and garnish with blueberries and almond leaves.

**NOTES**

_____
_____
_____
_____
_____

# Oriental Rice Pudding

**Ingredients for 3 servings:**
**Preparation time: approx. 20 minutes**

- 200 grams rice pudding
- 120 g dates, dried
- 50 g pistachio kernels, shelled
- 5 cardamon capsules or 1 teaspoon cardamon, ground
- 1 teaspoon cinnamon, ground
- 1 pulp of a vanilla pod
- 2 tablespoons honey
- 800 ml milk

### Preparation:

1. First, put the milk with the cardamom in a large pot. Crush the cardamon capsules in a mortar beforehand. The powder can be added directly to the milk.
2. Boil the milk briefly, add the rice and simmer over reduced heat for about 15 minutes. Stir regularly during this process.
3. Meanwhile, chop the pistachios and cut the dates into small cubes.
4. Pour 2/3 of the dates, cinnamon and vanilla pulp into the rice pudding and simmer gently for another 5-10 minutes. Continue to stir regularly.
5. When the rice is soft, sweeten with honey and stir in half of the pistachios.
6. Before serving, divide your rice pudding into three portions and garnish with the remaining date cubes and pistachios.

## NOTES

_____
_____
_____

# Delicious Birch Muesli

**Ingredients for 2 servings:**
**Preparation time: approx. 5 minutes / swelling time at least 8 hours**

- 6 tablespoons tender oat flakes
- 2 apples
- 2 bananas
- Juice of one lemon
- 1 pinch cinnamon, ground
- 2 tablespoons honey or agave syrup
- 2 tablespoons hazelnuts or almonds, chopped
- 100 ml cream or vegetable cream
- 240 ml milk or vegetable milk (e.g. almond milk)
- Topping: 2 tablespoons nuts, chopped, fruit (e.g. blueberries, strawberries)

**Preparation:**

1. Mix the oat flakes with the milk and let it swell covered in the fridge overnight.
2. The next morning, mash the bananas with a fork and grate the apples.
3. Stir bananas, apples, nuts, honey, cinnamon, cream and lemon juice into the swollen oat flakes.
4. Before serving, garnish your muesli with the topping of your choice.

**NOTES**

_____

_____

# Vegan Strawberry Banana Smoothie

### Ingredients for 2 servings:
### Preparation time: approx. 5 minutes

- 4 bananas
- 250 grams strawberries
- 1 pinch cinnamon, ground
- 1 tablespoon agave syrup
- 4 tablespoons linseed, coarsely ground
- 500 ml almond or rice milk

### Preparation:

1. Put all the ingredients in a blender and blend until creamy. If the smoothie is too thick, just add some milk and blend briefly.

# Raspberry Smoothie

### Ingredients for 2 servings:
### Preparation time: approx. 5 minutes

- 200 g frozen raspberries
- 1 pinch cinnamon, ground
- 2 tablespoons agave syrup or honey
- 2 tablespoons tender oat flakes
- 400 ml milk or vegetable milk

### Preparation:

1. Put all the ingredients in a blender and blend until creamy. If the smoothie is too thick, add a little more milk.

# Quinoa Breakfast Porridge

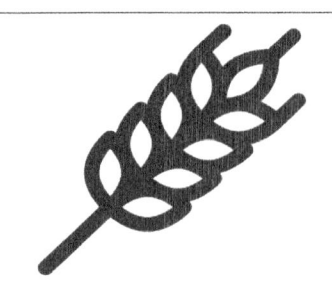

**Ingredients for 2 servings:**
**Preparation time: approx. 20 minutes**

- 100 grams quinoa
- 1 pinch cinnamon, ground
- 1 pulp of a vanilla pod
- 1 tablespoon honey or agave syrup
- 300 ml milk
- Topping: diced fruit, chopped nuts

**Preparation:**

1. First, rinse the quinoa in a sieve under running water.
2. Boil the milk with the cinnamon and vanilla pod in a saucepan, reduce the heat and stir in the quinoa. Simmer over medium heat for about 15 minutes until the quinoa is soft.
3. Take the pot off the cooker and let everything swell for about 5 minutes. Now stir in the honey or agave syrup, divide into two portions and garnish with the topping.

# Quick Semolina Porridge

**Ingredients for 2 servings:**
**Preparation time: approx. 10 minutes**

- 90 grams semolina
- 1 pinch cinnamon, ground
- 3 tablespoons sugar, honey or agave syrup
- 500 ml milk
- Topping: cocoa powder, butter

**Preparation:**

1. First, put the milk, semolina, cinnamon and sugar in a saucepan and simmer over medium heat until the mixture thickens. Keep stirring so that the porridge doesn't burn.
2. If the porridge is too thick, simply add a little more milk. If it is too liquid, stir in a little semolina and let the porridge swell a little.
3. Now divide the porridge into two portions and refine it with cocoa powder and butter. Best enjoyed hot.

# Breakfast Smoothie

**Ingredients for 1 serving:**
Preparation time: approx. 5 minutes

- 1 ripe banana
- 1 tablespoon tender oat flakes
- 1 tablespoon wheat germ
- 250 ml milk or vegetable milk

**Preparation:**

1. Put all the ingredients in a blender and blend until creamy. This smoothie is perfect if your child doesn't want to eat breakfast in the morning. You can add variety by varying the fruit. Use raspberries, strawberries, blueberries etc.

# Vegan Pick-Me-Up Smoothie

**Ingredients for 3 servings:**
Preparation time: approx. 30 minutes

- 1 ripe papaya
- 2 tablespoons chia seeds
- 1 pinch cinnamon, ground
- 1 tablespoon coconut blossom sugar
- 800 ml coconut rice drink
- 400 ml hazelnut drink

**Preparation:**

1. First, mix the hazelnut milk and the coconut rice milk with the quinoa. Add the cinnamon and coconut blossom sugar and stir well. Let everything soak for about 20 minutes, stirring in between.
2. In the meantime, peel the papaya, remove the seeds and cut it into small pieces.
3. Finally, put the papaya and the milk-quinoa mixture into a blender and blend until creamy.

# Good Morning Soup

**Ingredients for 1 serving:**
**Preparation time: approx. 15 minutes**

- 50 grams tender oat flakes
- 1 pinch of salt
- 2 tablespoons honey or agave syrup
- 300 ml milk

**Preparation:**

1. First, boil the milk. Reduce the heat and stir in the oat flakes, salt and honey and simmer for about 10 minutes. Stir regularly.
2. The soup will be rather thick. If you want it to be more liquid, add a little milk.

**NOTES**

_____
_____
_____
_____
_____
_____
_____
_____
_____
_____

# Crunchy Granola

**Ingredients for 10 servings:**
**Preparation time: approx. 25 minutes**

- 500 grams oat flakes
- 150 grams almonds, chopped
- 50 g vital seeds mix (sunflower, soy, pumpkin and pine nuts)
- 100 grams dried apples
- 1 pinch of salt
- 1 teaspoon cinnamon, ground
- 1 pulp of a vanilla pod
- 200 grams honey or agave syrup
- 170 grams coconut oil

**Preparation:**

1. First, preheat the oven to 180 degrees and line a baking tray with baking paper.
2. Then dice the apples and put them in a bowl with the oat flakes, nuts, seeds, salt, cinnamon and vanilla pulp.
3. Heat the honey and coconut oil in a pot. When the oil is liquid, pour the oil-honey mixture into the other ingredients and stir well.
4. Now spread your granola evenly on the baking tray. Bake for about 10 minutes, then use a spatula to turn the granola and bake for another 5 minutes. Check the oven from time to time to make sure the granola doesn't get too dark.
5. When it's ready, let it cool before pouring the granola into a container.
6. The granola will keep for at least 2 weeks. But since it's so delicious, it won't last that long at all.

# Mango Breakfast Lassi

**Ingredients for 2 servings:**
**Preparation time: approx. 5 minutes**

- 125 grams natural yoghurt
- 1 mango
- 2 tablespoons honey or agave syrup
- 1 teaspoon lemon juice
- 200 ml water

### Preparation:

1. First peel the mango, remove the core and cut into small cubes.
2. Now mix all the ingredients in a stand mixer until creamy.

# Green Power Smoothie

**Ingredients for 4 servings:**
**Preparation time: approx. 10 minutes**

- 1 handful baby spinach, roughly chopped
- 2 ripe bananas
- 1 Fennel
- 20 dates, without pit
- approx. 500 ml water

### Preparation:

1. First, cut the fennel into pieces and peel the bananas.
2. Put all the ingredients in a blender and blend well. Do not add all the water straight away, but blend first and if the smoothie is still too thick, add more water.

# Exotic Smoothie

**Ingredients for 2 servings:**
Preparation time: approx. 10 minutes

- 4 persimmons
- 2 oranges
- 2 bananas
- 2 tomatoes
- 1 Fennel
- 200 ml water

**Preparation:**

1. First, cut all the ingredients into pieces and blend in a blender until creamy. If the smoothie is still too thick, add a little more water.

# Red Good Mood Smoothie

**Ingredients for 2 servings:**
Preparation time: approx. 10 minutes

- 1 apple/ 1 carrot
- 1/2 piece beetroot, pre-cooked
- 1/4 mango
- 1/4 cucumber
- Juice of half a lemon
- approx. 1 cm long piece of ginger
- 1 teaspoon oil
- approx. 500 ml water

**Preparation:**

1. First peel the mango, carrot and ginger and cut them into small pieces. Cut the apple and cucumber into pieces and put all the ingredients into a blender. Do not add all the water straight away, but blend first and if the smoothie is still too thick, add more water.

# ONE POT
## VEGETARIAN & MORE

### ONE POT PASTA

40

# One Pot Pasta Viva Italia

**Ingredients for 2 servings:**
**Preparation time: approx. 30 minutes**

- 250 grams pasta (fusilli, farfalle, croissants, penne)
- 100 g spinach leaves, coarsely chopped
- 1 can tomatoes, chopped
- 1 onion
- 1 clove of garlic, pressed
- 2 teaspoons marjoram, chopped
- 1 handful basil, chopped
- 1 pinch chilli powder
- 1 pinch of salt and pepper
- 2 tablespoons olive oil
- 1 tablespoon cream cheese
- 375 ml vegetable stock

**Preparation:**

1. First peel and finely dice the onions.
2. Heat the oil in a large pot and sauté the onion and garlic until translucent.
3. Deglaze with the tomatoes, add the stock and pasta, season and simmer, covered, over a medium heat for about 20 minutes. Stir regularly and add a little stock if necessary.
4. Finally, stir in the spinach leaves and cream cheese and leave to stand for another 5 minutes.

## NOTES

_____

_____

_____

# Spring One Pot

### Ingredients for 4 servings:
### Preparation time: approx. 20 minutes

- 400 grams of pasta (short pasta such as penne)
- 500 grams green asparagus
- 3 tablespoons parsley, chopped
- 1 pinch of salt and pepper
- 1-2 tablespoons grated Parmesan cheese
- 500 ml vegetable stock

### Preparation:

1. First, wash the asparagus and cut it into pieces about 1 cm long. You do not need to peel green asparagus.
2. Then put all the ingredients, except for the asparagus and the Parmesan, into a large pot and bring to the boil. Then reduce the heat and simmer everything for about 10 minutes, add the asparagus pieces and let everything simmer on a low heat until the pasta is al dente. You can add more liquid if necessary. It's better if you don't use all the stock at the beginning, but keep adding a little at a time, because you want the sauce to be creamy. You can also refine the pot with a dash of white wine.
3. Before serving, add the Parmesan cheese, stir again and sprinkle with a little parsley.

**NOTES**

_____

_____

# Coconut One Pot Curry

### Ingredients for 2 servings:
**Preparation time: approx. 25 minutes**

- 250 grams linguine
- 2 pieces of pepper
- 1 carrot
- 1 bunch spring onion
- 1 clove of garlic, pressed
- 1 tablespoon curry powder
- 1 teaspoon salt
- nuts and basil to taste
- 1 can coconut milk
- 350 ml vegetable stock

### Preparation:

1. First peel the spring onion and cut it into thin rings.
2. Then wash and peel the carrot and the pepper and cut them into small pieces.
3. Then put all the ingredients, except for the nuts and basil, into a large pot and bring to the boil. Reduce the heat and simmer gently for about 10-15 minutes. Stir regularly.
4. Garnish with the nuts and basil before serving.

## NOTES

_____

_____

_____

_____

_____

# One Pot Pasta alla Napoletana

**Ingredients for 2 servings:**
**Preparation time: approx. 25 minutes**

- 250 grams pasta of your choice
- 1 can tomato pieces
- 1 small onion
- 1 clove of garlic, pressed
- 3 tablespoons tomato paste
- 1 pinch of salt and pepper
- 1 tablespoon basil, chopped
- 1 tablespoon Italian herbs, chopped
- 1 tablespoon olive oil
- 1 tablespoon balsamic vinegar
- 500 ml vegetable stock or water

**Preparation:**

1. First, finely dice the onion and sauté in a pot until translucent. Add the tomato paste and deglaze everything with the balsamic vinegar. Pour in the stock, add the penne, chopped tomatoes, herbs, salt and pepper and bring to the boil. Simmer over medium heat for about 10-15 minutes.
2. If you feel like it, you can pimp your One Pot by adding fresh vegetables or mixing in mozzarella.

**NOTES**

_____

_____

_____

_____

# One Pot Pasta al Funghi

**Ingredients for 4 servings:**
**Preparation time: approx. 45 minutes**

- 500 grams pasta of your choice
- 250 grams mushrooms
- 1 courgette
- 1 clove of garlic, pressed
- 4 sprigs thyme
- 1 sprig rosemary
- 1 pinch of salt and pepper
- 100 ml cream or vegetable cream
- 1500 ml vegetable stock or water

### Preparation:

1. First, cut the courgettes into small cubes (approx. 1 cm wide), then clean the mushrooms and cut them into slices. The best way to do this is to cut the mushrooms in half lengthwise and then slice them.
2. For thyme and rosemary, pluck the leaves from the branches.
3. Now you can add all the ingredients except the cream to the pot, bring to the boil and simmer over medium heat until the pasta is al dente. Remember to stir regularly.
4. Finally, add the cream and you're done.

# Spaetzle Vegetable One Pot

**Ingredients for 2 servings:**
Preparation time: approx. 20 minutes

- 300 g spaetzle, from the chiller cabinet
- 300 g frozen Kaiser vegetables
- 4 corners processed cheese
- 1 pinch of salt and pepper
- 2 tablespoons oil or butter
- A little milk to deglaze

### Preparation:

1. Heat the fat in a large frying pan and fry the spaetzle until brown.
2. Then add the vegetables and continue to sauté.
3. When everything is nice and crispy, deglaze with the milk.
4. Finally, add the processed cheese, season with salt and pepper and stir until the cheese is evenly mixed in.

# Thai One Pot Pasta

**Ingredients for 4 servings:**
**Preparation time: approx. 25 minutes**

- 500 grams pasta (short pasta such as farfalle)
- 1 red pepper
- 2 carrots
- 3 Spring onion
- 1 pinch of salt and pepper
- 1 teaspoon paprika powder, sweet
- 2 tablespoons peanut butter
- 20 grams ground peanuts
- 1 squeeze lime juice
- 100 ml cream or vegetable cream
- 1000 ml vegetable stock

**Preparation:**

1. Cut the peppers into small cubes and the spring onion into fine slices.
2. Grate the carrots.
3. Mix all the ingredients in a large saucepan, bring to the boil and simmer over medium heat until the pasta is al dente. Keep stirring regularly.

**NOTES**

_____
_____
_____
_____

# One Pot Vegetable Soup with Pasta

**Ingredients for 4 servings:**
**Preparation time: approx. 60 minutes**

- 200 grams pasta of your choice (e.g. Risoni or Gobbetti)
- 1 small cauliflower (approx. 400 g)
- 1 leek
- 4 carrots
- 1 kohlrabi
- 1/2 bulb celery
- 2 onions
- 4 tomatoes
- 3 cloves of garlic, pressed
- 4 tablespoons chives, chopped
- 1 pinch of salt and pepper
- 2 tablespoons oil to taste
- 1250 ml vegetable stock or water

**Preparation:**

1. First, chop the onions and dice the leek, celery and kohlrabi. Cut the carrots into slices. Divide the cauliflower into small florets and cut the tomatoes into small wedges.
2. Heat the oil in a large pot. Briefly sauté the onions, leeks, carrots, celery, cauliflower and kohlrabi.
3. Deglaze the vegetables with the stock and season with salt, pepper and garlic.
4. Add the pasta and bring to the boil. Cook over medium heat for about 10 - 15 minutes. The pasta should be al dente and the vegetables still a little crunchy.
5. Finally, stir in the tomatoes.
6. Garnish with the chives before serving.

# Colourful Pasta One Pot

**Ingredients for 2 people:**
Preparation time: approx. 20 minutes

- 120 grams pasta of choice (e.g. Mini Penne)
- 1 small onion
- 1 carrot
- 1 pepper, red
- 100 grams cocktail tomatoes
- 1 small can of corn
- 50 g frozen peas
- 1 tablespoon parsley, chopped
- 1 pinch paprika powder, sweet
- 1 pinch of salt and pepper
- 1 tablespoon oil to taste
- 100 ml milk
- 200 ml vegetable stock

**Preparation:**

1. Peel the onion and carrot and cut into small cubes. Also, dice the pepper, slice the tomatoes and drain the maize in a sieve.
2. Heat the oil in a large pot and fry the diced vegetables for about 3 minutes.
3. Deglaze with stock and milk. Add the peas and noodles, bring to the boil briefly and simmer over medium heat for about 10 minutes.
4. Now add the maize and season with salt, pepper and paprika powder.

## NOTES

_____

_____

_____

# One-Pot Tomato Pasta

### Ingredients for 2 servings:
### Preparation time: approx. 20 minutes

- 120 grams of pasta of your choice (small varieties are best)
- 150 g canned tomatoes, chopped
- 1 small onion
- 1 clove of garlic
- 10 cocktail tomatoes
- 2 tablespoons parmesan, grated
- 2 tablespoons parsley, chopped
- 1 pinch of salt and pepper
- 1 tablespoon olive oil
- 250 ml vegetable stock

### Preparation:

1. Peel and finely dice the onion and garlic. Halve or quarter the cocktail tomatoes (depends on the size).
2. Heat the oil in a large pot and sauté the onion and garlic until translucent. Then deglaze with the tinned tomatoes, add the stock and cook over a medium heat until the pasta is al dente.
3. Now add the cocktail tomatoes to the pot and season with salt, pepper and parsley.
4. Before serving, sprinkle the Parmesan over the top and your One-Pot Tomato Pasta is ready.

## NOTES

_____

_____

_____

# Alloy One Pot Noodle Soup

**Ingredients for 2 people:**
**Preparation time: approx. 30 minutes**

- 50 grams soup noodles
- 250 g vegetables (fresh or frozen, e.g. peas, carrots, kohlrabi, cauliflower)
- 1 Egg
- 4 tablespoons parsley, chopped
- 1 pinch of salt and pepper
- 1 tablespoon oil to taste
- 750 ml vegetable stock

**Preparation:**

1. First, prepare the vegetables if they are fresh (peel and dice).
2. Heat the oil in a large pot and fry the vegetables briefly.
3. Now deglaze with the vegetable stock and cook for about 5 minutes over medium heat.
4. Add the pasta, parsley, salt and pepper and simmer your pot again for about 5 minutes.
5. Take the pot off the cooker, break the egg into it and mix well. Let everything sit for a short time so that the egg sets.

## NOTES

_____

_____

_____

_____

_____

_____

# Tomato Spinach One Pot Pasta

**Ingredients for 2 servings:**
**Preparation time: approx. 20 minutes**

- 120 g pasta of your choice (e.g. mini farfalle)
- 4 small vine tomatoes
- 150 g leaf spinach, chopped (frozen or fresh)
- 1 small onion
- 1 clove of garlic
- 2 tablespoons parmesan, grated
- 1 pinch of salt and pepper
- 1 tablespoon olive oil
- 150 ml milk
- 150 ml vegetable stock

**Preparation:**

1. Peel and finely dice the onion and garlic, and also cut the tomatoes into small cubes.
2. Heat the olive oil in a large pot and sauté the onion and garlic until translucent before deglazing with the stock.
3. Now add the pasta, spinach and milk to the pot and bring to the boil over medium heat. Let everything simmer for about 10 minutes.
4. Finally, add the tomatoes, salt and pepper to the pot.
5. Before serving, sprinkle the Parmesan over the top and the delicious pasta is ready.

## NOTES

_____
_____
_____
_____

# Autumn Pumpkin One Pot

**Ingredients for 4 servings:**
**Preparation time: approx. 30 minutes**

- 500 g pasta (e.g. rigatoni)
- 1/2 Hokkaido pumpkin
- 1 small onion
- 1 clove of garlic, pressed
- 4 tablespoons parmesan, grated
- 1 pinch of salt and pepper
- 2 tablespoons olive oil
- 200 ml cream or vegetable cream
- 200 ml milk
- 700 ml vegetable stock

**Preparation:**

1. Peel and finely dice the onion, remove the seeds from the pumpkin with a spoon and cut into small cubes (you do not need to peel the Hokkaido pumpkin).
2. Heat the oil in a large pot and sauté the onion, garlic and pumpkin until translucent before deglazing with the vegetable stock.
3. Now add the milk, cream, pasta, salt and pepper to the pot and bring to the boil over medium heat. Let everything simmer until the pasta is al dente; stir occasionally.
4. Sprinkle the parmesan over the top before serving.

**NOTES**

_____
_____
_____
_____
_____

# Courgette Tomato One Pot

**Ingredients for 4 servings:**
**Preparation time: approx. 30 minutes**

- 500 g pasta (e.g. mini penne)
- 1 courgette
- 1 onion
- 2 cloves of garlic, pressed
- 10 cocktail tomatoes
- 2 packs of strained tomatoes
- 4 tablespoons parmesan, grated
- 1 pinch of salt and pepper
- 1 tablespoon basil, chopped
- 1 tablespoon oregano, chopped
- 2 tablespoons olive oil
- 100 ml cream or vegetable cream
- 400 ml vegetable stock

**Preparation:**

1. First, peel and finely dice the onion. Cut the tomatoes in half and the courgettes into small cubes.
2. Now, heat the oil in a large pot and sauté the onion, garlic and courgette until translucent.
3. Deglaze with the stock and add the pasta, strained tomatoes and cream and let everything simmer for about 15 minutes over medium heat. Stir in between every now and then.
4. When the pasta is al dente, season with salt, pepper, basil and oregano and add the cocktail tomatoes.
5. Stir everything again and sprinkle the Parmesan over the top before serving.

## NOTES

_____

_____

_____

# Mac 'n' Cheese One Pot

### Ingredients for 3 servings:
### Preparation time: approx. 20 minutes

- 500 grams macaroni
- 1 pinch of salt and pepper
- 1 pinch nutmeg
- 250 g cheese, grated (e.g. cheddar, mozzarella, parmesan)
- 3 tablespoons butter
- 250 ml cream or cooking cream
- 1000 ml milk

### Preparation:

1. Put the pasta, milk, cream and butter in a large pot and boil everything.
2. Simmer over medium heat for about 10 minutes until the pasta is al dente, stirring repeatedly.
3. Now stir in the cheese, season with salt, pepper and nutmeg and the cheese noodles are ready.

## NOTES

_____

_____

_____

_____

_____

_____

# Spinach Tomato One Pot Pasta

**Ingredients for 4 servings:**
**Preparation time: approx. 20 minutes**

- 500 grams spaghetti
- 1 courgette
- 1 onion
- 1 clove of garlic, pressed
- 100 g spinach leaves, coarsely chopped
- 10 cocktail tomatoes
- 50 grams dried tomatoes
- 4 tablespoons parmesan, grated
- 2 tablespoons cream cheese
- 1 pinch of salt and pepper
- 1 tablespoon oregano, chopped
- 2 tablespoons olive oil
- 250 ml cream or vegetable cream
- 750 ml vegetable stock

**Preparation:**

1. First, peel and finely dice the onion. Cut the dried tomatoes into small pieces.
2. Heat the oil in a large pot and sauté the onion and garlic until translucent. Add the tomatoes and spinach and sauté briefly.
3. Deglaze with the stock and cream and add the pasta, boil briefly and simmer for about 10 minutes over a medium heat. Stir in between.
4. When the pasta is al dente, season with salt, pepper and oregano and add the cocktail tomatoes, cream cheese and Parmesan. Stir well and serve.

# Mushroom One Pot Pasta with Gorgonzola

**Ingredients for 4 servings:**
**Preparation time: approx. 45 minutes**

- 350 grams pasta (e.g. penne)
- 350 grams brown mushrooms
- 2 onions
- 3 cloves of garlic, pressed
- 180 grams Gorgonzola
- 1 pinch of salt and pepper
- 3 tablespoons oil to taste
- 200 ml cream or vegetable cream
- 600 ml vegetable stock

**Preparation:**

1. First peel and finely dice the onion. Clean the mushrooms, halve them and cut them into thin slices. Dice the gorgonzola.
2. Now heat the oil in a large pot and sauté the onions, garlic and mushrooms until translucent.
3. Deglaze with the stock and cream and add the pasta. Bring everything to the boil and simmer for about 10 minutes over medium heat. In between, you have to stir often.
4. When the pasta is al dente, season with salt, pepper and oregano and stir in the Gorgonzola.

## NOTES

_____

_____

_____

_____

_____

# One Pot Pasta alla Caprese

**Ingredients for 4 people:**
**Preparation time: approx. 30 minutes**

- 500 grams fusilli
- 125 grams mozzarella
- 1 onion
- 2 cloves of garlic, pressed
- 1 jar of dried tomatoes, preserved in oil
- 75 grams parmesan, grated
- 1 pinch of salt and pepper
- 1 bunch basil
- 2 tablespoons olive oil
- 250 ml cream or vegetable cream
- 750 ml vegetable stock

**Preparation:**

1. First, peel and finely dice the onion. Chop the dried tomatoes into small pieces. (You can keep the oil from the tomatoes and use it for salads).
2. Cut the mozzarella into small cubes and roughly chop the basil leaves. Leave a few of the leaves on the side to garnish later.
3. Now heat the olive oil in a large pot and sauté the onion and garlic until translucent.
4. Deglaze with the stock and add the cream, pasta and tomatoes, bring everything to the boil briefly and then simmer for about 10 - 15 minutes over medium heat. Stir again and again in between.
5. Take the pot off the cooker and add the mozzarella and Parmesan. Season with salt and pepper and leave to stand for a short time.
6. Stir well again and garnish with the basil leaves set aside before serving.

# One Pot Pasta alla Genovese

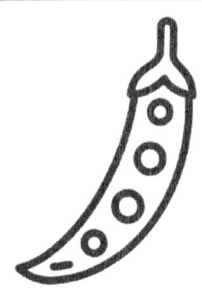

**Ingredients for 2 servings:**
**Preparation time: approx. 30 minutes**

- 200 grams linguine
- 200 grams frozen princess beans
- 1 potato, waxy
- 1 onion, white
- 1 clove of garlic, pressed
- 1 pinch of salt and pepper
- 1 jar Pesto alla Genovese
- 2 tablespoons olive oil
- 600 ml vegetable stock
- To garnish: 4 tablespoons basil, chopped

**Preparation:**

1. First, peel and finely chop the onions, then peel and dice the potatoes.
2. Now, heat the olive oil in a large pot. Sauté the onion and garlic until translucent, add the potatoes and beans and sauté briefly.
3. Deglaze with the stock, add the pasta and simmer over a medium heat for about 10 minutes.
4. When your pasta is al dente, stir in the pesto and season with salt and pepper.
5. Before serving, sprinkle the Parmesan over the top and garnish with the basil leaves.

## NOTES

_____

_____

_____

_____

_____

# Pasta-Vegetable-One-Pot

**Ingredients for 3 servings:**
**Preparation time: approx. 25 minutes**

- 500 grams of pasta (penne, farfalle or other small pasta)
- 150 grams broccoli
- 1 pointed pepper
- 1 courgette
- 1 carrot
- 4 cocktail tomatoes
- 2 spring onions
- 2 cloves of garlic, pressed
- 1 pinch of salt and pepper
- 2 tablespoons oil to taste
- 250 ml cream or vegetable cream
- 500 ml vegetable stock

**Preparation:**

1. First, peel and finely dice the spring onion. Peel the courgette and carrot and cut into small cubes or slices. Cut the peppers into strips and the broccoli into florets. Halve the cocktail tomatoes.
2. Heat the oil in a large pot and sauté the onions and garlic until translucent. Add the courgettes, carrots and broccoli and fry them briefly as well.
3. Deglaze with stock and cream, add the pasta, salt and pepper and simmer over a medium heat until the pasta is al dente.
4. Before serving, fold in the cocktail tomatoes and leave to stand for a few minutes.

**NOTES**

# Fried Thai Noodles One Pot

**Ingredients for 3 servings:**
**Preparation time: approx. 10 minutes**

- 200 grams Thai noodles
- 150 g vegetable mix (peppers, carrots, broccoli)
- 6 cloves of garlic, pressed
- 4 tablespoons peanut butter
- 2 tablespoons chilli sauce, hot
- 1 pinch of salt and pepper
- 2 tablespoons coconut oil
- 1 can coconut milk

### Preparation:

1. First prepare the Thai noodles according to the instructions.
2. Heat the coconut oil in a large pot and sauté the vegetables and garlic until translucent.
3. Now add the rest of the ingredients to the pot and simmer for about 5 minutes on a low heat.
4. Season again before serving, add more seasoning if necessary or water to dilute.

# Broccoli One Pot Pasta

**Ingredients for 2 servings:**
**Preparation time: approx. 20 minutes**

- 80 grams pasta (e.g. rigatoni)
- 200 g frozen broccoli
- 100 g frozen peas
- 100 grams mushrooms
- 1 handful rocket
- 2 onions, red
- 90 grams cream cheese
- 2 eggs, soft boiled
- 2 pinches turmeric, ground
- 1 pinch of salt and pepper
- 1 tablespoon Worcester sauce
- 300 ml vegetable stock

### Preparation:

1. First peel and chop the onions. Clean the mushrooms and cut them into slices.
2. Now put the vegetable stock, turmeric, noodles, onions and mushrooms into a large pot. Bring to the boil once and simmer over medium heat for about 7 minutes.
3. Add the peas and broccoli and simmer for another 5 minutes.
4. Now stir in the cream cheese and season your pot with salt, pepper and Worcester sauce.
5. Divide into two portions and spread evenly on the rocket. Peel the eggs, carefully halve them and place them on the rocket.

# Exotic Coconut Tomato One Pot Pasta

## Ingredients for 4 servings:
**Preparation time: approx. 20 minutes**

- 400 grams linguine
- 300 g leaf spinach, coarsely chopped
- 200 g frozen peas
- 2 cans tomatoes, chopped
- 2 peppers, red
- 2 onions, white
- 4 cloves of garlic, pressed
- 40 grams ginger, finely chopped
- 60 grams coconut chips, roasted
- 2 pinches turmeric, ground
- 1 pinch of salt and pepper
- Juice of one lime
- 2 cans coconut milk
- 600 ml vegetable stock

## Preparation:

1. First, peel and finely dice the onions and cut the pepper into strips.
2. Put the noodles, onions, garlic, peppers, peas, tomatoes, stock and coconut milk in a large pot, bring to the boil once and simmer over medium heat for about 12 minutes. Stir regularly.
3. Before serving, fold the spinach into the pasta, season with lime juice and garnish with the coconut chips.

**NOTES**

_____
_____
_____
_____

# Peanut Ginger One Pot Pasta

### Ingredients for 2 servings:
Preparation time: approx. 25 minutes

- 250 g spaghetti (e.g. wholemeal spelt spaghetti)
- 1 small broccoli
- 1 pepper, red
- 10 grams ginger
- 2 cloves of garlic, pressed
- Pinch of salt and pepper
- 1 tablespoon peanut oil
- 2 tablespoons nori seaweed
- 3 tablespoons peanut butter
- 6 tablespoons soy sauce
- 600 ml stock vegetable stock
- For garnish: Sesame

### Preparation:

1. First peel and chop the ginger, dice the pepper and divide the broccoli into florets.
2. Heat the oil in a large pot and sauté the garlic and ginger until translucent. Sauté the pepper and broccoli briefly as well, then deglaze with stock.
3. Now add the noodles and salt to the pot and let everything simmer, covered, for about 15 minutes over medium heat.
4. Now, add the seaweed soy sauce and peanut butter to the spaghetti, stir well and season a little if necessary.
5. Before serving, sprinkle sesame seeds over the pasta.

**NOTES**

_____

_____

_____

_____

# ONE POT

## VEGETARIAN & MORE

### ONE POT MAIN DISHES

# Quinoa Vegetable One Pot

**Ingredients for 4 servings:**
**Preparation time: approx. 30 minutes**

- 200 grams quinoa
- 200 grams feta
- 200 g leaf spinach, coarsely chopped
- 2 sweet potato
- 2 avocados
- 2 onions
- 2 cloves of garlic, pressed
- 1 pinch of salt and pepper
- 1 pinch nutmeg, grated
- 2 tablespoons olive oil
- 500 ml vegetable stock

**Preparation:**

1. First, peel and finely dice the onions. Peel the sweet potatoes and avocados as well and cut into small cubes.
2. Heat the oil in a large pot, sauté the onion and garlic until translucent, fry the sweet potato cubes briefly and add the quinoa.
3. Deglaze with the vegetable stock, season everything with salt, pepper and nutmeg and let your pot simmer, covered, for about 20 minutes over medium heat. Stir regularly and add a little water if necessary.
4. Finally, fold in the spinach and avocado and sprinkle the crumbled feta over your quinoa pot.

**NOTES**

_____
_____
_____
_____
_____
_____
_____

# Pumpkin Lentil Chili sin Carne

**Ingredients for 4 servings:**
**Preparation time: approx. 60 minutes**

- 500 grams Hokkaido pumpkin
- 200 grams beluga lentils
- 1 can tomatoes, strained
- 2 chilli peppers, finely chopped
- 1 onion
- 1 clove of garlic, pressed
- 1 teaspoon cinnamon
- 1 teaspoon turmeric
- 1 teaspoon paprika powder, sweet
- 1/2 teaspoon cumin, ground
- 1 pinch of salt and pepper
- 2 tablespoons coconut oil
- Juice of one lime
- 1 teaspoon maple syrup
- 2 tablespoons soy sauce
- 1 can coconut milk
- To garnish: 4 tablespoons parsley, chopped

**Preparation:**

1. First, prepare the lentils according to the instructions on the packet.
2. Peel the onion and chop finely. Cut the pumpkin into small cubes (you do not need to peel the Hokkaido pumpkin).
3. Now, heat the coconut oil in a large pot. Sauté the onion and garlic until translucent. Fry the diced pumpkin and chilli for a few minutes over a medium heat.
4. Deglaze with the strained tomatoes, add the already cooked lentils, soy sauce, maple syrup and spices. Let your chilli simmer for about 15 minutes. Stir regularly so that nothing burns.
5. Before serving, refine with coconut milk and lime juice. Season a little more if necessary. Divide into four portions and garnish with parsley.

# Oriental Rice One Pot

**Ingredients for 3 servings:**
**Preparation time: approx. 30 minutes**

- 200 grams basmati rice
- 300 grams potatoes, waxy
- 1 can tomatoes, chopped
- 2 small onions, white
- 1 tablespoon turmeric
- 1 teaspoon cayenne pepper
- 1 teaspoon cumin, ground
- 1 pinch of salt and pepper
- 2 tablespoons coconut oil
- 400 ml vegetable stock
- For garnish: 4 tablespoons yoghurt, 3 tablespoons coriander, chopped

**Preparation:**

1. Peel the onion and chop finely. Also peel the potato and cut into small cubes.
2. Now heat the coconut oil in a large pot, sauté the onion until translucent, add the spices and potato cubes and sauté for about 3 minutes. Deglaze with the tomatoes, stir in the rice and stock and let everything simmer gently over a low heat for about 15 minutes.
3. Before serving, divide into three portions and garnish with yoghurt and coriander.

## NOTES

_____
_____
_____
_____
_____
_____

# Greek Style Rice One Pot

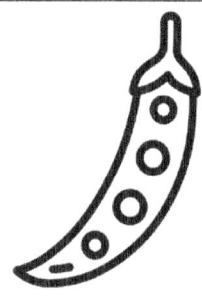

Ingredients for 3 servings:
Preparation time: approx. 25 minutes

- 250 grams basmati rice
- 150 grams feta
- 1 small tin of chickpeas
- 1 pepper, red
- 1 aubergine
- 1 onion
- 2 cloves of garlic, pressed
- 3 tablespoons tomato paste
- 3 tablespoons frozen herb mix
- 1 pinch of salt and pepper
- 2 tablespoons coconut oil
- 700 ml vegetable stock
- For garnish: Parsley, chopped

### Preparation:

1. Peel and finely chop the onion. Cut the aubergine and pepper into small cubes. Drain the chickpeas in a sieve.
2. Now heat the coconut oil in a large pot. Sauté the onion and garlic until translucent, add the diced aubergine and peppers and sauté for about 3 minutes.
3. Stir in the tomato paste, deglaze with stock, add the rice and spices. Simmer over medium heat for about 10 minutes. Then add the chickpeas to the pot and cook for another 5 minutes.
4. Finally, crumble the feta, stir into the pot and garnish with chopped parsley before serving.

## NOTES

_____
_____
_____
_____

# Indian Lentil Dhal One Pot

**Ingredients for 3 servings:**
**Preparation time: approx. 35 minutes**

- 250 g lentils, orange
- 2 sweet potatoes
- 80 grams leaf spinach coarsely chopped
- 4 spring onions
- 1 clove of garlic, pressed
- 1 chilli pepper, red
- 1 piece of fresh ginger, peeled (approx. 3 cm in size)
- 1 level tablespoon turmeric
- 1 level tablespoon cumin, ground
- 1 pinch of salt
- 1 tablespoon sesame oil
- 600 ml vegetable stock
- For garnish: 4 tablespoons Thai basil

## Preparation:

1. First, peel the onions and cut them into slices. Also peel the sweet potatoes and cut into small cubes. Finely chop the chilli and ginger. Rinse the lentils in a sieve under running water.
2. Heat the oil in a large pot, sweat the onions, garlic and chilli until translucent.
3. Now add the sweet potatoes, lentils, deglaze with the stock and let everything simmer over medium heat for about 20 minutes.
4. Fold in the spinach leaves and season with salt, turmeric and cumin.
5. Before serving, garnish your Indian dhal with the basil leaves.

# Potato Spinach One Pot Curry

**Ingredients for 4 servings:**
**Preparation time: approx. 60 minutes**

- 1000 grams potatoes, waxy
- 200 grams spinach, coarsely chopped
- 1 can tomatoes, chopped
- 1 tablespoon ginger, grated
- 1 bunch coriander leaves
- 1 chilli pepper, red, finely chopped
- 1/2 teaspoon cumin, whole
- 1 teaspoon cumin, ground
- 1 pinch turmeric
- 1 pinch of salt and pepper
- 1 tablespoon garam masala
- 2 tablespoons coconut oil
- 600 ml vegetable stock
- For garnish: 1 tablespoon coriander, chopped

**Preparation:**

1. First, peel the potatoes and cut into small cubes.
2. Now puree the tomatoes, ginger, chilli pepper and coriander (including the stems) in a blender.
3. Heat the coconut oil in a large pot and fry the cumin until brown. Add the pureed tomato mix, turmeric, cumin powder, salt, pepper and garam masala. Simmer everything over medium heat for about 3 minutes.
4. Now, add the potatoes and the stock and let everything simmer for about 40 minutes. Stir regularly.
5. Then add the spinach to the pot and let everything simmer for a short while. Add a little salt if necessary.
6. Divide into four portions and garnish with coriander leaves before serving.

# Low Carb One Pot

**Ingredients for 2 servings:**
**Preparation time: approx. 25 minutes**

- 2 courgettes, medium
- 250 grams cocktail tomatoes
- 1 onion, red
- 1 clove of garlic, pressed
- 1 bunch basil, coarsely chopped
- 1 pinch of salt and pepper
- 1 pinch chilli powder
- 30 grams grated parmesan
- 3 tablespoons olive oil
- To garnish: 4 basil leaves

### Preparation:

1. First, peel and finely chop the onion and halve the tomatoes.
2. Cut the courgettes into strips with a spiral slicer.
3. Heat the oil in a large pot and sauté the onions and garlic until translucent.
4. Add the courgette noodles and steam for approx. 2-3 minutes over a medium heat.
5. Season with chilli powder, salt and pepper.
6. Finally, fold in the Parmesan cheese and tomatoes. Garnish with basil

## NOTES

_____

_____

_____

_____

_____

_____

# Chana Masala One Pot

**Ingredients for 4 servings:**
**Preparation time: approx. 25 minutes**

- 2 cans chickpeas
- 2 cans tomatoes, chopped
- 2 onions, white
- 2 peppers, red
- 4 tablespoons tomato paste
- 2 tablespoons cumin, ground
- 1 tablespoon curry powder
- 1 pinch chilli powder
- 1 pinch of salt and pepper
- 2 tablespoons olive oil
- For garnish: 4 tablespoons yoghurt, a few leaves of coriander

**Preparation:**

1. First, peel and finely dice the onions and cut the pepper into strips.
2. Heat the olive oil in a large pot and sauté the onions and peppers until translucent.
3. Stir in the tomato paste, fry briefly and deglaze with the tomatoes.
4. Add the chickpeas and spices and simmer over reduced heat for about 15 minutes.
5. Season to taste before serving, adding salt and pepper if necessary.
6. Divide into four portions, garnish with yoghurt and coriander leaves and serve immediately.

## NOTES

___
___
___
___
___

# Oriental Lentil Rice One Pot

### Ingredients for 3 servings:
**Preparation time: approx. 60 minutes**

- 100 grams brown rice
- 100 grams mountain lentils
- 30 g frozen peas
- 1 sweet potato
- 2 onions, white
- 3 cloves of garlic, pressed
- 1 tablespoon ginger, grated
- 1 bay leaf
- 1 tablespoon cumin, ground
- 1 tablespoon curry powder
- 1/2 teaspoon cinnamon, ground
- 1 pinch allspice, ground
- 1 pinch cayenne pepper
- 1 pinch of salt and pepper
- Juice of half a lemon
- 2 tablespoons olive oil
- 500 ml vegetable stock
- For garnish: 3 tablespoons yoghurt, a few leaves of coriander, 3 teaspoons pine nuts

### Preparation:

1. First, peel and finely dice the onions. Also peel the sweet potato and cut into cubes.
2. Heat the olive oil in a large pot and sauté the onions, garlic and sweet potato until translucent.
3. Deglaze with the stock, add the rice, lentils, bay leaf and ginger and simmer gently over a low heat for about 25-30 minutes.
4. Add the peas and spices and simmer for another 10 minutes until everything is soft.
5. Season to taste before serving, adding salt and pepper if necessary.
6. Divide into three portions and drizzle the lemon juice evenly over the top.
7. Garnish with yoghurt and coriander leaves before serving.

# Risotto with Lemon and Celery

**Ingredients for 4 servings:**
**Preparation time: approx. 35 minutes**

- 500 grams risotto rice
- 200 grams parmesan, grated
- 2 onions, white
- 4 cloves of garlic, pressed
- 2 stalks celery
- 1 pinch of salt and pepper
- Juice and grated lemon
- 6 tablespoons olive oil
- 75 ml cream or vegetable cream
- 1750 ml vegetable stock

**Preparation:**

1. First, peel and finely dice the onions and finely slice the celery.
2. Heat the oil in a large pot. Sauté the onions, garlic and celery until translucent, add the rice and deglaze with stock.
3. Gradually pour in the stock and simmer on a low heat for about 20 minutes. It is important to stir constantly and only add enough stock to cover the rice.
4. When the risotto is cooked, remove the pot from the cooker. Now add the cream, spices, lemon zest and lemon juice.
5. Finally, stir in the Parmesan cheese and leave the risotto to stand for about 5 minutes.

**NOTES**

_____
_____
_____
_____
_____
_____

# Simple Vegetable Rice

**Ingredients for 4 servings:**
**Preparation time: approx. 25 minutes**

- 180 grams rice
- 200 g frozen pea-carrot mixture
- 1 small can of corn
- 1 pepper, red
- 8 mushrooms
- 1 small onion
- 2 tablespoons frozen herb mix
- 1 pinch of salt and pepper
- 2 tablespoons oil to taste
- 400 ml vegetable stock

### Preparation:

1. First, peel and finely dice the onions. Also dice the peppers and mushrooms. Drain the maize in a sieve.
2. Heat the oil in a large pot. Sauté the onion, pepper and mushrooms until translucent, add the rice and deglaze with the stock.
3. Let your pot simmer on medium heat for about 10 minutes. Stir regularly.
4. Add the frozen mixture, sweetcorn and herbs, stir well and leave to infuse for another 5 minutes.
5. Season with salt and pepper before serving.

# Rice One Pot alla Genovese

**Ingredients for 4 servings:**
**Preparation time: approx. 20 minutes**

- 150 grams rice
- 1 cup mini mozzarella
- 1 courgette
- 1 small onion
- 1 pinch of salt and pepper
- 4 tablespoons pesto genovese
- 1 tablespoon oil to taste
- approx. 350 ml vegetable stock

### Preparation:

1. First, peel and finely chop the onions. Cut the courgettes into cubes.
2. Heat the oil in a large pot. Sauté the onion and courgette until translucent, add the rice and deglaze with the stock.
3. Simmer over medium heat for about 10 minutes. Stir regularly.
4. Remove the pan from the heat, add the mozzarella balls, salt and pesto and leave to stand for about 5 minutes.

# One-Pot Risotto

**Ingredients for 4 servings:**
**Preparation time: approx. 40 minutes**

- 250 grams risotto rice
- 100 grams parmesan, grated
- 2 tablespoons tomato paste
- 2 peppers, yellow and red
- 1 onion, white
- 2 cloves of garlic, pressed
- 100 grams cashew nuts, ground
- 1 pinch of salt and pepper
- 1 pinch rosemary, rubbed
- 2 tablespoons olive oil
- 500 ml vegetable stock

### Preparation:

1. First, peel and finely chop the onions. Cut the peppers into small cubes.
2. Heat the oil in a large pot. Sauté the onion, garlic and pepper until translucent, add the tomato paste and rice and deglaze with the stock.
3. Gradually pour in the stock and simmer on a low heat for about 20 minutes. It is important to stir constantly and only add enough stock to cover the rice.
4. When the risotto is cooked, remove the pot from the cooker. Now add the ground nuts and spices.
5. Finally, stir in the Parmesan cheese and leave the risotto to stand for about 5 minutes.

# Pumpkin Polenta One Pot

**Ingredients for 4 servings:**
**Preparation time: approx. 20 minutes**

- 200 grams polenta (corn semolina)
- 200 grams butternut squash
- 1 onion, white
- 1 teaspoon paprika powder, sweet
- 1 pinch of salt and pepper
- 1 tablespoon butter
- 2 tablespoons parmesan, grated
- 2 tablespoons oil to taste
- 500 ml milk/ 500 ml vegetable stock

### Preparation:

1. First, peel and finely chop the onions. Cut the pumpkin into small cubes.
2. Heat the oil in a large pot. Sauté the onion until translucent, add the paprika powder. Deglaze with milk and stock, bring to the boil, stir in polenta with a whisk and leave to swell over a low heat for about 10 minutes. Stir regularly.
3. Now fold in the pumpkin cubes and cook for another 5 minutes.
4. Before serving, divide into four portions and garnish with Parmesan cheese and butter flakes.

# One-Pot Ratatouille

### Ingredients for 2 servings:
Preparation time: approx. 30 minutes

- 150 g potatoes, waxy
- 50 grams chickpeas
- 1 pepper, yellow
- 1 tomato
- 1 small courgette
- 1 small onion, white
- 100 grams feta
- 200 grams yoghurt
- 1 pinch of salt and pepper
- 1 tablespoon olive oil
- approx. 100 ml vegetable stock
- To garnish: 1 tablespoon frozen herb mix

### Preparation:

1. First, peel and finely chop the onions. Cut the potatoes, courgettes, peppers and tomatoes into small cubes. You can crumble the feta by hand.
2. Heat the oil in a large pot. Sauté the onions, potatoes and peppers until translucent.
3. Now add the diced tomatoes and chickpeas and deglaze with the stock.
4. Let the pot simmer gently over medium heat for about 10-15 minutes. The potatoes should be cooked.
5. Finally, season the ratatouille, fold in the yoghurt and feta and garnish with the herbs.

# Vegetable Egg One Pot

### Ingredients for 2 servings:
Preparation time: approx. 60 minutes

- 400 grams potatoes, waxy
- 450 grams frozen vegetables, ready cooked
- 2 eggs
- 1 pinch of salt and pepper
- 4 tablespoons oil to taste
- approx. 30 ml mineral water
- To garnish: 1 tablespoon parsley, chopped

### Preparation:

1. First, peel the potatoes and cut them into slices.
2. Heat the oil in a large pot and fry the potatoes in it until crispy, season with salt and pepper.
3. Now, add the vegetables and continue to fry for about 2 minutes over a medium heat.
4. Whisk the eggs with the mineral water, then pour the mixture over the vegetables.
5. When the eggs have set, stir well and season if necessary.
6. Arrange on plates and garnish with the parsley.

# Potato-Broccoli-One-Pot

**Ingredients for 2 servings:**
Preparation time: approx. 35 minutes

- 250 g potatoes, floury
- 350 grams broccoli
- 1 teaspoon thyme, dried
- 1 teaspoon marjoram, dried
- 1 pinch of salt and pepper
- 1 tablespoon potato starch
- 1 tablespoon butter
- 250 ml vegetable stock
- To garnish: 1 tablespoon chives, chopped

**Preparation:**

1. First, cut the potatoes into small cubes and divide the broccoli into florets.
2. In a large pot, boil the potatoes, broccoli and vegetable stock and simmer over medium heat for about 15 minutes.
3. Then stir in the butter and salt, pepper and spices.
4. Mix the potato starch with a little water in a cup and pour it into the pot.
5. If the consistency is still too thin, simply add a little more starch.
6. Finally, season a little more if necessary and garnish with the chives.

# Carrot and Potato Puree

**Ingredients for 4 servings:**
Preparation time: approx. 35 minutes

- 400 grams potatoes, floury
- 400 grams carrots
- 1 pinch of salt and pepper
- 1 tablespoon parsley, chopped
- 1 pinch nutmeg, grated
- 4 tablespoons olive oil
- 2 tablespoons butter
- 2 tablespoons milk
- 600 ml vegetable stock

**Preparation:**

1. First, peel and dice the carrots and potatoes.
2. Heat the oil in a large pot. Sauté the potatoes and carrots until translucent.
3. Then deglaze with the stock, bring to the boil and simmer over a medium heat for about 20 minutes.
4. Now stir in the milk and parsley and puree with a hand blender.
5. Before serving, stir in the butter and season with nutmeg.

# Delicious Vegetable Cream One Pot

**Ingredients for 2 servings:**
Preparation time: approx. 20 minutes

- 300 grams potatoes, waxy
- 300 grams cauliflower
- 1 pinch of salt and pepper
- 1 pinch paprika powder, sweet
- 4 tablespoons cream cheese
- 300 ml vegetable stock

### Preparation:

1. First, peel the potatoes and cut them into small cubes. Divide the cauliflower into small florets.
2. Bring stock to the boil in a large pot, add potatoes and cauliflower and simmer gently over medium heat for about 15 minutes.
3. Now add the cream cheese and season with salt and pepper.
4. Arrange on plates and garnish with the paprika powder.

# One Pot Gnocchi in Tomato Sauce

**Ingredients for 2 servings:**
Preparation time: approx. 20 minutes

- 200 g gnocchi, from the chiller cabinet
- 200 g canned tomatoes, chopped
- 1 pepper, red
- 1 small onion, white
- 1 tablespoon tomato paste
- 1 tablespoon basil, chopped
- 1 pinch of salt and pepper
- 1 tablespoon butter
- 100 ml milk

### Preparation:

1. First peel and finely chop the onion. Cut the pepper into small cubes.
2. Heat the butter in a large saucepan and sauté the onions and peppers until translucent.
3. Add the tomato paste and gnocchi, fry over a medium heat for about 2 minutes, then deglaze with the milk.
4. Now add the diced tomatoes, season with salt, pepper and basil and cook for about 5 minutes.

# Thai Curry One Pot Gnocchi

**Ingredients for 4 servings:**
Preparation time: approx. 30 minutes

- 800 grams gnocchi, from the chiller cabinet
- 100 grams bamboo shoots
- 1 pepper, red
- 1 courgette
- 1 carrot
- 1 onion, white
- 2 cloves of garlic, pressed
- 2 tablespoons curry paste, yellow
- 1 pinch of salt and pepper
- 1 can coconut milk
- 2 tablespoons coconut oil
- 150 ml vegetable stock

## Preparation:

1. First, peel and finely chop the onion. Cut the peppers, carrots and courgettes into small cubes.
2. Heat the coconut oil in a large saucepan and sauté the onion, garlic, pepper and carrot until translucent.
3. Now, stir in the curry paste, salt and pepper, add the gnocchi and deglaze with stock and coconut milk. Simmer gently over medium heat for approx. 5 - 7 minutes. Stir regularly.

# Gnocchi One Pot Caprese

**Ingredients for 4 servings:**
Preparation time: approx. 20 minutes

- 1000 grams gnocchi, from the chiller cabinet
- 1 cup mini mozzarella
- 2 cans tomatoes, chopped
- 1 onion
- 1 clove of garlic, pressed
- 30 grams basil, chopped
- 2 tablespoons tomato paste
- 1 pinch of salt and pepper
- 1 tablespoon cane sugar
- 3 tablespoons olive oil
- 200 ml vegetable stock

## Preparation:

1. First, peel and finely chop the onion.
2. Heat the oil in a large pot and sweat the onion and garlic until translucent.
3. Now, stir in the sugar, let it caramelise briefly, add the tomato paste and deglaze with the diced tomatoes and the stock.
4. Add the gnocchi and simmer over a medium heat for about 5 minutes.
5. Add the mozzarella, basil, salt and pepper and stir until the mozzarella has melted.

# One Pot Curry with Cauliflower

### Ingredients for 4 servings:
### Preparation time: approx. 40 minutes

- 1000 grams potatoes, waxy
- 900 grams cauliflower
- 2 onions
- 4 cloves of garlic, pressed
- 1 teaspoon cumin, ground
- 2 tablespoons curry powder
- 1 pinch of salt and pepper
- 1 teaspoon mustard
- 1 tablespoon lemon juice
- 2 tablespoons coconut oil
- 1 can coconut milk
- 500 ml vegetable stock

### Preparation:

1. First peel the onion and chop finely. Peel and chop the potatoes as well. Divide the cauliflower into small florets.
2. Heat the oil in a large pot and sweat the onions and garlic until translucent.
3. Add the potatoes, cauliflower, mustard, cumin and curry powder, sauté for two minutes and deglaze with coconut milk.
4. Stir in the stock, salt, pepper and lemon juice and simmer on a medium heat, covered, for about 20 minutes. Stir regularly.

# Leek and Potato One-Pot

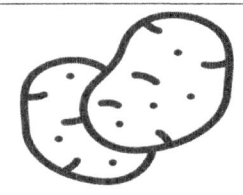

### Ingredients for 4 servings:
### Preparation time: approx. 50 minutes

- 800 grams potatoes, waxy
- 350 grams leek
- 1/2 teaspoon pepper
- 1 tablespoon salt
- 50 grams flour
- 50 grams butter
- 200 ml milk
- 150 ml cream

### Preparation:

1. First peel the potatoes and cut them into small cubes. Wash the leeks and cut them into rings.
2. Heat the butter in a large pot and sauté the leeks until translucent. Add the potatoes and fry briefly.
3. Deglaze with the milk, stir in the flour and simmer gently over a low heat for about 10-15 minutes. Stir regularly.
4. Now stir in the cream and season with salt and pepper. Remove from the heat and leave to stand for about 5 minutes.

# Veggie Yakisoba One Pot

**Ingredients for 2 servings:**
Preparation time: approx. 30 minutes

- 250 g yakisoba noodles (Japanese noodles)
- 1 pepper, red
- 1 small head of broccoli
- 2 carrots
- 1 onion
- 1/2 teaspoon pepper
- 1 tablespoon salt
- 4 tablespoons Worcester sauce
- 2 tablespoons soy sauce
- 2 tablespoons oyster sauce
- 2 tablespoons sugar
- 2 tablespoons coconut oil

### Preparation:

1. First prepare the pasta according to the package instructions.
2. Peel and chop the onion. Cut the broccoli into small florets, cut the pepper into strips and slice the carrots.
3. For the yakisoba sauce, put salt, pepper, sugar, Worcester, soy and oyster sauce in a bowl and mix well.
4. Heat the oil in a large pot and sauté the vegetables until translucent.
5. Now add the noodles and yakisoba sauce to the pot. Simmer gently over medium heat for about 5 minutes. Stir regularly.

# One-Pot Vegetable Spaetzle

**Ingredients for 2 servings:**
Preparation time: approx. 20 minutes

- 1 pack of spaetzle, from the chiller cabinet
- 1 pack frozen buttered vegetables
- 150 grams processed cheese
- 1 pinch of salt and pepper
- 2 tablespoons butter
- Milk for deglazing

### Preparation:

1. Heat the butter in a large saucepan, fry the spaetzle over a medium heat for about 3 minutes until crispy and deglaze with milk.
2. Add the buttered vegetables, stir in the processed cheese, season with salt and pepper, remove from the heat and leave to stand for about 5 minutes.

# Courgette Noodles Alla Carbonara

### Ingredients for 3 servings:
**Preparation time: approx. 25 minutes**

- 800 grams courgettes
- 125 grams cooked ham
- 100 grams processed cheese
- 20 grams parmesan, grated
- 1 onion
- 1 pinch of salt and pepper
- 1 tablespoon olive oil
- 2 cups sour cream

### Preparation:

1. First peel and finely chop the onion. Cut the ham into small cubes.
2. Cut the courgettes into strips with a spiral slicer.
3. Heat the oil in a large pot and sauté the onions until translucent.
4. Add the courgette noodles and sauté for about 2-3 minutes over a medium heat.
5. Stir in the sour cream, Parmesan and processed cheese and cook for another 2 minutes.
6. Season with salt and pepper before serving.

## NOTES

_____
_____
_____
_____
_____
_____
_____

# Mediterranean Style Quinoa Salad

## Ingredients for 2 servings:

Preparation time: approx. 35 minutes

- 200 grams quinoa
- 200 grams mushrooms
- 2 tomatoes
- 1/2 cucumber
- 1 onion
- 16 black olives, pitted
- 2 tablespoons Italian herb mix
- 2 tablespoons basil, chopped
- Pinch of salt and pepper
- 2 tablespoons Vital Seeds Mix
- 1 squeeze lemon juice
- 3 tablespoons olive oil
- 3 tablespoons balsamic vinegar
- 450 ml vegetable stock

## Preparation:

1. First, finely chop the onion, clean the mushrooms and slice them. Rinse the quinoa well in a sieve under running water.
2. Heat 1 tablespoon of oil in a pot and sauté the onion until translucent. Sauté the mushrooms briefly as well.
3. Now, add the quinoa to the pot, fry briefly and deglaze with vegetable stock. Cover and simmer over medium heat for about 15 minutes. Then remove from the cooker and leave to swell, covered, for about 5 minutes. Then leave to cool in a bowl.
4. In the meantime, cut the cucumber and tomatoes into small cubes and halve the olives.
5. Add the chopped vegetables together with 2 tablespoons of oil, lemon juice, balsamic vinegar, herbs, salt, pepper and the seed mix to the quinoa and stir well.
6. Garnish the salad with the basil before serving.
7. Tip: For a more intense flavour, you can fry the seeds briefly in a coated pan.

**NOTES**

# Exotic One Pot Coconut Lentil Curry

### Ingredients for approx. 3 servings:
### Preparation time: approx. 30 minutes

- 200 grams yellow lentils
- 2 waxy potatoes
- 2 carrots
- 1 broccoli
- ½ fennel
- 1 onion
- 1 clove of garlic, pressed
- 10 grams fresh ginger
- 2 tablespoons curry powder
- 1 teaspoon cumin seeds
- 1 teaspoon coriander seeds
- 1 teaspoon fennel seeds
- 1 tablespoon turmeric powder
- 1 pinch of salt and pepper
- 2 tablespoons coconut puree
- 2 tablespoons coconut oil
- 2 tablespoons soy sauce
- 1 tablespoon lemon or lime juice
- 500 ml water
- To garnish: 1 handful of cashews and 1 sprig of fresh coriander

### Preparation:

1. First, peel and chop the onion and ginger.
2. Peel and slice the carrots and potatoes. Wash the broccoli and cut it into small florets, cut the fennel into thin slices.
3. Heat the oil in a large pot and sauté the onion, garlic, ginger and seeds until translucent. Deglaze with water, add salt, pepper and turmeric and puree with a hand blender - this is the creamy base for the curry.
4. Now, add the prepared vegetables and the washed lentils to the pot. Cover and simmer for about 20 minutes over medium heat.
5. Now add soy sauce, coconut puree and lemon juice, stir well and serve in soup bowls.
6. Pluck the leaves off the coriander and toast the cashews a little in a non-stick frying pan.
7. Before serving, garnish your curry with coriander leaves and cashews.

# Oriental Millet One Pot

### Ingredients for 2 servings:
**Preparation time: approx. 30 minutes**

- 200 grams millet
- 2 carrots
- 1 pepper, red
- 1 courgette
- 1 onion
- 8 dates
- 8 apricots, dried
- 45 grams almonds
- 1 pinch of salt and pepper
- 1 teaspoon cinnamon, ground
- 1 tablespoon cumin seeds, ground
- 2 tablespoons parsley, chopped
- 2 tablespoons almond paste
- 2 tablespoons oil to taste
- 1 tablespoon balsamic vinegar
- 700 ml vegetable stock

### Preparation:

1. First chop the onions and almonds, then cut the peppers, courgettes and carrots into small cubes. Rinse the millet in a sieve under running water.
2. Heat the oil in a large pot, sweat the onions and almonds until translucent, add the diced vegetables and fry everything briefly.
3. Now add the millet, cumin seeds and cinnamon, deglaze with the broth and let everything simmer on a medium heat, covered, for about 15 minutes. Then remove from the heat and leave the millet to swell for another 5 minutes.
4. Finely dice the apricots and dates and mix with the millet together with the balsamic vinegar, almond paste, salt and pepper.
5. Sprinkle with the parsley before serving.

**NOTES**

_____

_____

_____

# Millet-Amaranth-One-Pot

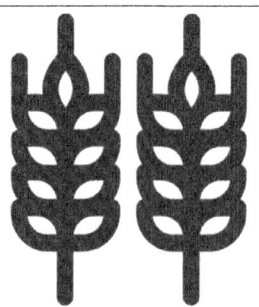

### Ingredients for 2 servings:
**Preparation time: approx. 40 minutes**

- 100 grams amaranth
- 100 grams millet
- 200 grams cauliflower
- 1 carrot
- 1/2 pepper, red
- 1 stalk of celery
- 1 onion
- 1 clove of garlic, pressed
- 2 teaspoons salt
- 1/2 teaspoon cumin seeds, ground
- 1/2 teaspoon chilli powder
- 1/2 teaspoon pepper
- 2 tablespoons coriander, chopped
- 2 tablespoons almond paste
- 2 tablespoons coconut oil
- 500 ml vegetable stock

### Preparation:

1. First, chop the onion, pepper, carrot and celery into small cubes. Cut the broccoli into small florets. Rinse the millet and amaranth in a sieve under running water.
2. Heat the oil in a large pot, sauté the onions until translucent, add the diced vegetables and fry everything briefly.
3. Now, add the millet and amaranth, deglaze with the broth, add the spices and let everything simmer on a medium heat, covered for about 15 minutes. Then remove from the cooker and leave to swell for about 5 minutes.
4. Garnish with the coriander before serving.

**NOTES**

_____

_____

_____

# One Pot Rice with Vegetables

## Ingredients for 2 servings:
**Preparation time: approx. 30 minutes**

- 160 grams rice
- 200 grams cocktail tomatoes
- 1 fennel bulb
- 2 small white onions
- 2 bunches spring onions
- 1 clove of garlic, pressed
- 1 pinch of salt and pepper
- 1 pinch chilli powder
- 1 teaspoon thyme
- 1 tablespoon parsley, chopped
- Juice of one lemon
- 1 tablespoon oil to taste
- 450 ml vegetable stock

## Preparation:

1. First, chop the onion finely and cut the fennel into thin strips. Set the green part of the fennel aside.
2. Heat the oil in a large pot, sweat the onions, garlic and fennel until translucent, add the rice and deglaze with the stock. Simmer over medium heat for about 10 minutes.
3. In the meantime, chop the spring onion and fennel greens and halve the tomatoes.
4. Once the rice is cooked, add the rest of the vegetables and season with lemon juice and spices.
5. Garnish with parsley before serving.

**NOTES**

# Quinoa Tofu One Pot

### Ingredients for 3 servings:
**Preparation time: approx. 35 minutes**

- 250 grams quinoa
- 200 grams smoked tofu
- 1 small can of corn
- 1 tin kidney beans
- 2 onions
- 1 clove of garlic, pressed
- 100 grams tomato paste
- 1 tablespoon salt
- 1 tablespoon paprika powder, sweet
- 1 teaspoon cocoa powder
- 1 teaspoon cumin, ground
- 1 teaspoon oregano
- 1 pinch chilli powder
- 2 tablespoons maple syrup or agave syrup
- 2 tablespoons balsamic vinegar
- 500 ml vegetable stock
- For garnish 3 tablespoons parsley, chopped

### Preparation:

1. First, rinse the quinoa well in a sieve under running water. For maize and beans, pour off the juice.
2. Cut the smoked tofu into small cubes and chop the onion.
3. Put all the ingredients in a large saucepan, bring to the boil briefly and simmer over a medium heat for about 15 minutes.
4. Before serving, garnish your pot with the chopped parsley.

# Potato Salad One Pot

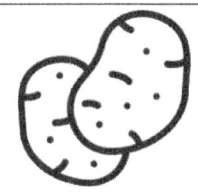

**Ingredients for 4 servings:**
Preparation time: approx. 90 minutes
- 1000 grams potatoes, waxy
- 2 onions
- 2 cloves of garlic, pressed
- 1 pinch of salt and pepper
- 1 teaspoon sugar
- 1 teaspoon mustard
- 2 tablespoons parsley, chopped
- 8 tablespoons oil to taste
- approx. 150 ml vegetable stock

### Preparation:

1. First peel the potatoes and cut them evenly into thin slices. Finely chop the onions.
2. Heat 75 ml of stock in a large pot, add the onions and potato slices and cook over a low heat for about 15 minutes. Stir in between.
3. After 15 minutes, check whether the potatoes are already cooked. If they are still too hard, add a little more stock. It is important not to add all the stock at once.
4. Remove the pot from the cooker, let it cool a little and mix in the mustard, oil, sugar and parsley.
5. Leave to cool before serving

# Asian Rice Noodle One Pot

**Ingredients for 4 servings:**
**Preparation time: approx. 25 minutes**

- 180 grams rice noodles
- 2 pieces pak choi
- 200 grams mushrooms
- 200 grams sugar snap peas
- 4 cm piece of ginger, chopped
- 2 onions, chopped
- 6 cloves of garlic, pressed
- 2 tablespoons cane sugar
- 2 limes
- 4 tablespoons soy sauce
- 1 tablespoon hot chilli sauce
- 1 tablespoon sesame oil
- 4 tablespoons peanut oil
- 125 ml vegetable stock

### Preparation:

1. First cut the pak choi into strips, clean the mushrooms and quarter them.
2. Heat the peanut oil in a wok. Fry the onions, garlic and ginger. Briefly fry the mushrooms and pak choi, sugar snap peas. Deglaze with soy sauce and stock.
3. Now add the remaining ingredients to the wok and let everything simmer, covered, over a low heat for about 5 minutes.
4. Mix well before serving and garnish with the coriander.

# Vegan Carrot One Pot Risotto

## Ingredients for 4 servings:
**Preparation time: approx. 45 minutes**

- 300 grams risotto rice
- 4 stalks celery
- 1000 grams carrots
- 200 grams sugar snap peas
- 2 onions
- 4 garlic cloves
- 8 sprigs thyme
- 1 teaspoon sea salt, coarse
- 1 pinch of pepper
- 1 tablespoon agave syrup
- 6 tablespoons olive oil
- 100 ml grape juice
- approx. 700 ml vegetable stock

## Preparation:

1. First, preheat the oven to 220 degrees top/bottom heat.
2. Peel the carrots, cut them into quarters lengthwise and place them on a baking tray lined with baking paper.
3. Spread the garlic with its peel and 4 sprigs of thyme on the baking tray. Sprinkle the agave syrup and sea salt evenly over the carrots. Cook in the oven for about 30 minutes until the carrots are soft.
4. In the meantime, peel and finely dice the onions. Cut the celery into thin slices.
5. Heat the oil in a large pot and sauté the onions and celery until translucent. Add the rice and the remaining thyme sprigs and sauté briefly. Reduce the heat, deglaze with grape juice and gradually pour the stock into the pot. The rice should only be slightly covered with the stock. Keep stirring and adding the stock until the rice is al dente. Remove the thyme sprigs. Then remove the pot from the cooker and cover the rice and let it cook.
6. Now put half of the soft carrots into a container, squeeze the garlic out of the skin, add it to the carrots and puree with a hand blender.
7. Add the pureed carrots to the risotto, season with salt and pepper and stir well.
8. Before serving, divide into four portions and serve with the remaining carrots.

# Vegan Bulgur Salad

**Ingredients for 4 servings:**
Preparation time: approx. 50 minutes
- 200 grams bulgur
- 1 bunch spring onion
- 3 tomatoes
- 1 bunch flat-leaf parsley, chopped
- 1/2 bunch mint, chopped
- 1 tablespoon tomato paste
- 1 pinch of salt and pepper
- 1/2 teaspoon paprika powder, hot
- 1 teaspoon cumin, ground
- Juice of one lemon
- 3 tablespoons olive oil
- 300 ml vegetable stock

### Preparation:

1. First, boil the bulgur together with the stock, remove from the heat and leave to soak for about 30 minutes.
2. Now chop the spring onion and tomatoes into small cubes.
3. Put the cooled bulgur in a bowl and mix in the tomatoes and onions.
4. Make a marinade with the tomato paste, lemon juice, oil, paprika powder, cumin, salt and pepper. Mix the marinade with the bulgur and leave to soak for about 20 minutes.

# Vegan Rice Pudding

**Ingredients for 3 servings:**
Preparation time: approx. 50 minutes
- 180 grams rice pudding
- 40 grams cane sugar
- 1 star anise
- 1 stick cinnamon/ 1 pinch salt
- 1 vanilla pod, halved lengthwise
- 1 litre almond drink (milk)
- Topping: e.g. cinnamon, cocoa, apple sauce, stewed cherries

### Preparation:

1. Boil the almond milk with the sugar, salt and all the spices. Reduce the heat, stir in the rice and leave to soak over a low heat for about 45 minutes. Stir regularly.
2. Remove the cinnamon stick, vanilla pod and star anise and divide the rice pudding into three portions. Garnish with toppings of your choice before serving.

# Vegan Lentil Bolognese One Pot for Kids

### Ingredients for 4 servings:
**Preparation time: approx. 45 minutes**
- 200 grams lentils, red
- 2 carrots
- 1 courgette
- 1 can tomatoes, chopped
- 2 tablespoons tomato paste
- 1 pinch of salt and pepper
- 1 teaspoon thyme
- 1 teaspoon oregano
- 1 bag fennel tea
- 1 tablespoon olive oil
- 250 ml vegetable stock

### Preparation:
1. First finely dice the vegetables, heat the oil in a pot and sauté the vegetables until translucent.
2. Stir in the tomato purée, sauté briefly and deglaze with the tinned tomatoes.
3. Add the stock, lentils, spices and the bag with the fennel seeds to the pot and simmer for about 25 minutes over medium heat.
4. Before serving, season again and remove the tea bag.

# Colourful Salad

### Ingredients for 4 children:
**Preparation time: approx. 15 minutes**
- 3 carrots/ 1 apple
- 1 small can of corn
- 1/2 cucumber
- 1 pinch of salt and pepper
- 1 pinch of mustard
- Juice of half a lemon
- 2 tablespoons oil to taste
- 1 tablespoon apple cider vinegar

### Preparation:
1. First, cut the cucumber and apple into small cubes. Grate the carrots. Drain the maize in a sieve.
2. Mix the fruit and vegetables in a bowl.
3. Make a vinaigrette with the lemon juice, vinegar, oil, mustard, salt and pepper.
4. Pour the vinaigrette into the bowl, stir everything well and let it sit for about 5 minutes.
5. Season again before serving. If the salad is too spicy, add a little water.

# Tofu Vegetable One Pot

## Ingredients for 2 servings:
**Preparation time: approx. 30 minutes**

- 100 grams smoked tofu
- 150 grams broccoli
- 100 grams carrots
- 1 pepper, red
- 3 onions, red
- 1 clove of garlic, pressed
- 1 pinch of salt and pepper
- 2 tablespoons frozen herb mix
- 1 tablespoon coconut oil
- 200 ml soy cream
- To garnish 2 tablespoons parsley, chopped

## Preparation:
1. Cut the smoked tofu and peppers into small cubes. Cut the onions into wedges and the carrots into thin slices. Cut the broccoli into florets.
2. Heat the coconut oil in a large pot and fry the tofu until crispy.
3. Now, add all the vegetables to the pot, fry them briefly and deglaze everything with the soy cream. Cover and simmer over medium heat for about 10 minutes.
4. Now, add salt, pepper and the herbs and simmer for another 5 minutes. Stir regularly.
5. Before serving, garnish your pot with the chopped parsley.

**NOTES**

# Chili-sin-Carne-con-Soja

## Ingredients for 4 servings:
**Preparation time: approx. 40 minutes**

- 150 grams soy granules
- 2 cans tomatoes, chopped
- 1 can corn
- 1 tin kidney beans
- 1 onion
- 3 cloves of garlic, pressed
- 3 tablespoons tomato paste
- 1 tablespoon salt
- 1 tablespoon paprika powder, sweet
- 1 pinch cayenne pepper
- 1 pinch of pepper
- 1/2 teaspoon cumin, ground
- 1 teaspoon oregano
- 1 teaspoon cane sugar
- 2 pieces cooking chocolate
- 2 tablespoons coconut oil
- 100 ml soy cream
- 100 ml vegetable stock
- To garnish 2 tablespoons parsley, chopped

## Preparation:

1. First, prepare the soy granules according to the instructions on the packet.
2. Finely dice the onions. Drain the maize and kidney beans in a sieve.
3. Heat the oil in a large pot and sauté the onion and garlic until translucent. Add the sugar and tomato paste and sauté briefly.
4. Now add the finished soy granules to the pot, fry them vigorously for a short time and deglaze everything with the stock and the canned tomatoes. Add the corn and beans and simmer on a low heat for about 15 minutes.
5. Now add salt, pepper, herbs and the chocolate and simmer for another 5 minutes. Stir regularly.
6. Before serving, garnish your chilli sin carne with the chopped parsley.

# Vegan Vegetable Curry

## Ingredients for 4 servings:
**Preparation time: approx. 35 minutes**

- 300 grams broccoli
- 3 Peppers, red
- 4 cloves of garlic, pressed
- 1 piece ginger (1 cm)
- 1 tablespoon curry powder
- 1 tablespoon salt
- 1/2 teaspoon turmeric powder
- 1 pinch chilli powder
- 1 pinch of pepper
- 1 teaspoon lemon juice
- 1 teaspoon agave syrup
- 1 teaspoon cornflour
- 1 tablespoon water
- 2 tablespoons coconut oil
- 400 ml coconut milk

## Preparation:

1. First, peel and finely chop the ginger. Cut the broccoli into florets and the pepper into small cubes.
2. Heat the oil in a large pot and sauté the ginger and garlic until translucent. Add the pepper and broccoli and fry briefly. Deglaze with coconut milk, stir in the spices and simmer for about 10 minutes over medium heat.
3. To thicken the sauce, mix the starch with the water and stir in the pot. If the curry is still too thin, simply add a little more starch/water mixture.
4. Now add salt, pepper, herbs and the chocolate and simmer for another 5 minutes. Stir regularly.
5. Season with lemon juice and agave syrup before serving.

**NOTES**

# Moroccan Quinoa One Pot

## Ingredients for 6 servings:
**Preparation time: approx. 45 minutes**

- 340 grams quinoa
- 1000 grams sweet potato
- 300 g leaf spinach, coarsely chopped
- 2 cans chickpeas
- 2 carrots
- 1 pepper, yellow
- 1 small fennel
- 1 can tomatoes, chopped
- 1 onion
- 3 cloves of garlic, pressed
- 1 teaspoon paprika powder, sweet
- 1 teaspoon cumin powder
- 1 teaspoon turmeric powder
- 1 teaspoon coriander
- 1 pinch cinnamon
- 1 pinch cayenne pepper
- 1 pinch of salt and pepper
- Juice of one lemon
- 1 teaspoon apple cider vinegar
- 2 tablespoons olive oil
- 750 ml vegetable stock
- To garnish: fresh herbs (e.g. mint or parsley), chopped

## Preparation:

1. First, peel and finely chop the onion. Peel the sweet potato and carrots and cut into cubes. Cut the pepper, fennel and kale into small pieces.
2. Prepare the quinoa according to the instructions on the packet.
3. Heat the oil in a large pot, sauté the onion and garlic until translucent, add the spices and fry briefly.
4. Now add the sweet potato, pepper, carrots and fennel and sauté for another two minutes over medium heat.
5. Deglaze with stock, add tomatoes and bring to the boil briefly. Simmer at medium for about 15-20 minutes until the potatoes are soft.
6. Add the chickpeas to your pot and simmer for another 10 minutes.
7. Finally, add the quinoa and spinach leaves, season with vinegar and lemon juice, stir and add a little salt if necessary.
8. Garnish with the fresh herbs before serving.

# One-Pot Quinoa Bowl

### Ingredients for 3 servings:
**Preparation time: approx. 40 minutes**

- 180 grams quinoa
- 1 small tin of kidney beans
- 1 small can of corn
- 1 small tin of peas
- 1 pepper, orange
- 1 ripe avocado
- 2 cloves of garlic, pressed
- 2 tablespoons coriander leaves, chopped
- 2 tablespoons tomato paste
- 1 pinch paprika powder, sweet
- 1 pinch chilli powder
- 1 pinch of salt and pepper
- 1/2 teaspoon cumin
- Juice of half a lemon
- 1 tablespoon olive oil
- 750 ml vegetable stock

### Preparation:

1. First, dice the pepper and cut the chilli pepper into fine strips. Rinse the quinoa in a sieve under running water. Drain the beans, maize and peas.
2. Heat the oil in a large pot, sauté the garlic and chilli until translucent, add the tomato paste and sauté briefly.
3. Now add the quinoa and deglaze with the stock. Add the peppers, corn, beans, peas and spices to the pot and simmer, covered, for about 20 minutes over medium heat.
4. Finally, halve, pit and peel the avocado and cut into slices. Fold the avocado into the bowl together with the lime juice and coriander leaves.

**NOTES**

_____

_____

# ONE POT

## VEGETARIAN & MORE

# SNACKS

# Sheet Pan Kale Chips

### Ingredients for 4 servings:
**Preparation time: approx. 50 minutes**

- 250 grams kale
- 1 teaspoon chilli flakes, dried
- 2 teaspoons herb salt
- 40 ml olive oil

### Preparation:
1. First, preheat the oven to 130 degrees.
2. Wash the kale, dry it and remove the stalk. Cut the kale into bite-sized pieces (not too small, the kale shrinks in the oven).
3. Mix the oil with the salt and chilli flakes in a bowl and toss the kale pieces. The kale should be well covered with the oil.
4. Now spread the pieces on a baking tray covered with baking paper. Bake in the preheated oven for approx. 30 - 40 minutes. Open the oven door from time to time so that the steam can escape.
5. The chips are also delicious when served with a herb dip.

# Fresh Goat Cheese and Melon Salad

### Ingredients for 4 servings:
**Preparation time: approx. 20 minutes**

- 1000 grams watermelon
- 150 grams goat's cream cheese
- 20 grams basil
- 1 pinch of salt and pepper
- Juice of half a lemon
- 1 tablespoon honey
- 16 ml olive oil

### Preparation:
1. First, cut the watermelon into small cubes and the basil leaves into fine strips. Put both in a bowl.
2. Crumble the cheese and add to the bowl.
3. For the vinaigrette, mix the oil, honey and lemon juice, season with salt and pepper.
4. Add the vinaigrette to the melons and cheese and leave to infuse for a few minutes.

# Vanilla Cinnamon Almond Snack

### Ingredients for 2 servings:

- 50 g almonds
- 1 tablespoon coconut oil
- 1 tsp ground vanilla
- 1 pinch cinnamon

### Preparation:

1. Heat 1 tsp coconut oil in a pan.
2. Toast the almonds for 3 minutes over medium heat. Add the cinnamon and ground vanilla, mix together and roast for about 1 minute.
3. Leave the roasted almonds to cool on a baking tray lined with baking paper.
4. Enjoy as a delicious snack.

# Chips Low Carb

### Ingredients for 12 chips:

- 4 egg white
- 50 g parmesan
- Salt
- Pepper
- Any other spices (e.g. chilli flakes)

### Preparation:

1. Separate the eggs and grate the cheese. Mix the egg whites with the spices. Use sparingly here, as spices are difficult to mix with eggs. (do not beat until foamy)
2. Pour the egg whites into muffin cups. Sprinkle grated cheese on top of the egg whites.
3. Bake at 180 degrees top/bottom heat for approx. 12-15 minutes until golden brown.
4. If the cheese rises in the ramekins, simply cool and allow to collapse.

# Cheese Balls

### Ingredients for 9 balls:

- 30 g Italian herbs frozen or fresh
- 100 g cream cheese
- 100 g feta
- ½ tsp salt
- 1 tsp pepper
- 1 tsp curry

### Preparation:

1. Put all the ingredients in a bowl. Crumble the feta.
2. Then mash the mixture with a fork and mix thoroughly.
3. Then form small balls with your hands.
4. Place the balls on a plate and store in the fridge until ready to eat.

# Hummus with Vegetable Sticks

### Ingredients for 2 servings:

- 300 g canned chickpeas
- 1 garlic clove
- Juice of 1/2 lemon
- 2 tbsp olive oil
- 2 tbsp tahini (sesame paste)
- Salt/ Pepper
- 1 tsp chilli powder
- 1 tsp paprika powder

**Sticks:**
- 1 carrot/ 1 cucumber
- 1 stalk of celery

### Preparation:

1. Drain the chickpeas from the tin and add the lemon juice and garlic cloves and puree everything together.
2. Once everything is well pureed, add the sesame seeds. Season to taste with salt, pepper, paprika powder and chilli powder.
3. For dipping, wash and clean the vegetables and cut into strips.

# Sesame Sunflower Crackers

## Ingredients for 20 crackers:

- 125 g sunflower seeds
- 70 g sesame seeds
- 1 clove of garlic
- 1 tbsp dried herbs (e.g. rosemary)
- 3-5 tbsp. water
- 1 tablespoon olive oil
- ¼ tsp salt

## Preparation:

1. Preheat the oven to 180 degrees top and bottom heat.
2. Grind the sunflower seeds, salt and garlic in a blender or food processor on high speed for a few minutes until the whole thing looks slightly flour-like.
3. Add the sesame seeds, herbs and olive oil and mix on a low heat.
4. Add water by the spoonful until the mixture reaches a doughy consistency.
5. Roll out on a baking tray with baking paper. It is best to place another sheet of baking paper on top of the dough and then flatten with a rolling pin. Cut into pieces with a knife.
6. Bake for 10-15 minutes or until the crackers are lightly brown around the edges.
7. Allow to cool completely and then break apart.

# ONE POT
## VEGETARIAN & MORE

## DESSERT

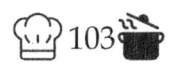

# Coconut Semolina Porridge

**Ingredients for 2 servings:**
Preparation time: approx. 20 minutes

- 150 grams semolina
- 2 tablespoons honey or sugar
- 400 ml coconut milk
- 200 ml water
- For garnish: 2 tablespoons grated coconut

### Preparation:

1. Boil the coconut milk and water in a saucepan and reduce the heat.
2. Stir in the honey and semolina and let everything simmer while stirring until the porridge becomes more solid.
3. Serve in two bowls and garnish with grated coconut.

## Chocolate Nut Cookie One Pot

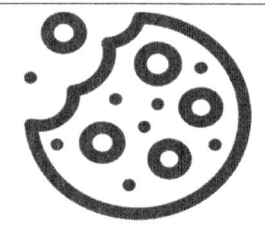

**Ingredients for 2 servings:**
Preparation time: approx. 30 minutes

- 100 grams butter
- 100 grams flour, plain
- 100 grams cane sugar
- 50 grams chocolate drops
- 50 grams hazelnuts, chopped
- 1 tablespoon vanilla sugar
- 1 teaspoon baking powder
- 1 pinch of salt
- 1 Egg

### Preparation:

1. Preheat the oven to 170 degrees.
2. In a wide saucepan or deep pan (coated), melt the butter and allow to cool briefly.
3. Remove the pan from the heat and whisk in the sugar and egg.
4. Add the flour, salt and baking powder.
5. Fold in the nuts and chocolate drops, stir well. Put the pan in the oven and bake for about 20 minutes.

# After-Eight Chocolate Cream

### Ingredients for 4 servings:
**Preparation time: approx. 10 minutes**

- 4 ripe avocados
- 4 ripe bananas
- 3 sprigs mint
- 120 grams cocoa powder
- 2 tablespoons honey or agave syrup
- For garnish: 4 tablespoons nuts, chopped

### Preparation:

1. First, peel the avocados and bananas and puree them together with the mint leaves using a hand blender.
2. Stir in the cocoa powder and honey.
3. Leave to infuse in the fridge for at least one hour.
4. Garnish with chopped nuts before serving.

# Berry Semolina Porridge

### Ingredients for 3 servings:
**Preparation time: approx. 15 minutes**

- 140 grams semolina
- 200 g frozen berry mix
- 2 ripe bananas
- 2 tablespoons honey or agave syrup
- 600 ml milk or vegetable milk (e.g. almond milk)

### Preparation:

1. First, put the milk and honey in a saucepan, bring to the boil briefly and stir in the semolina. Simmer over reduced heat, stirring, for about 5 minutes.
2. Peel the banana and mash it with a fork. Then fold the banana into the semolina porridge.
3. Divide the semolina porridge into four portions. Garnish with berries before serving.

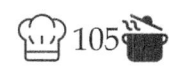

# Banana Chia Pudding

## Ingredients for 2 servings:
**Preparation time: approx. 3 hours with cooling time**

- 90 grams chia seeds
- 2 ripe bananas
- 2 tablespoons honey or agave syrup
- 3 tablespoons cocoa powder
- 400 ml milk or vegetable milk (e.g. rice-coconut drink)
- To garnish: 1 handful of berries

## Preparation:

1. First, mix the milk, cocoa and honey in a bowl and stir in the chia seeds.
2. Peel the banana and cut into thin slices. Fold into the mixture and leave to soak in the fridge for at least 3 hours.
3. Divide the pudding into two portions and garnish with the berries before serving.

# Vanilla Pudding with Chocolate Sauce

## Ingredients for 6 servings:
**Preparation time: approx. 20 minutes**

- 90 grams cornflour
- 60 grams sugar
- 2 vanilla beans
- 800 ml milk
- For the sauce: 160 g cooking chocolate, 200 ml milk

## Preparation:

1. First stir the cornflour into 100 ml milk.
2. Cut the vanilla pods lengthwise and scrape out the pith.
3. Put the remaining milk (700 ml) together with the sugar, vanilla pod and pulp into a saucepan and bring to the boil. Remove the pod, take the saucepan off the heat and reduce the heat. Add the starch-milk mixture, stirring constantly. Use a sieve to prevent lumps from forming.
4. Simmer the pudding for another 3 minutes at reduced heat, stirring constantly.
5. While the pudding is cooling, whip the cream until stiff, then fold into the cold pudding.
6. For the chocolate sauce, chop the chocolate into pieces and heat in a saucepan with the milk until the chocolate has melted.
7. Divide the pudding into six portions and garnish with the sauce before serving.

# Crispy Low Carb Cinnamon Wafers

### Ingredients for 6 pieces:
**Preparation time: approx. 30 minutes**

- 45 grams almond flour
- 60 grams birch sugar
- 50 grams butter, liquid
- 1 tablespoon cinnamon, ground
- 1/2 teaspoon baking powder
- 5 eggs
- approx. 20 ml milk
- Butter for the waffle iron
- To garnish: finely chopped fruit and birch icing sugar

### Preparation:

1. First, heat the waffle iron so that it is nice and hot.
2. Mix the flour, sugar, baking powder, butter, eggs, milk and cinnamon in a bowl until smooth.
3. Set the waffle iron to medium heat and grease with butter.
4. Now - depending on the waffle iron - pour approx. 2-3 tablespoons of batter into the waffle iron.
5. Bake the waffles for about 3-5 minutes until golden brown.
6. Before serving, garnish the waffles with some fruit and icing sugar.

# Express Dessert Chocolate Banana

### Ingredients for 4 servings:
**Preparation time: approx. 5 minutes**

- 4 bananas
- 2 tablespoons baking cocoa
- 2 tablespoons honey or agave syrup
- 2 tablespoons water

### Preparation:

1. First, cut the bananas lengthwise and place the banana halves on a plate.
2. Now mix the baking cocoa with the water, slowly stirring in the water. Add the honey to this sauce. Pour the chocolate sauce over the banana halves and heat in the microwave for about 10 seconds. Your lightning dessert is ready.

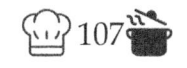

# Vegan Raw Food Dessert

### Ingredients for 4 servings:
**Preparation time: approx. 15 minutes**

- 4 apples
- 4 carrots
- Juice from 2 oranges
- 2 tablespoons agave syrup
- 1 tablespoon oil to taste
- 1 tablespoon fine oat flakes
- For garnish: 1 orange

### Preparation:

1. First, peel and finely grate the carrots, then finely grate the apples.
2. Mix the grated carrots and apples with the orange juice, oil, honey and oat flakes in a bowl.
3. Peel the orange and cut it into thin slices.
4. Garnish with the sliced orange before serving.

# Colourful Fruit Island

### Ingredients for 4 servings:
**Preparation time: approx. 10 minutes**

- 8 blueberries
- 4 kiwis
- 2 bananas
- 2 oranges
- some lemon juice

### Preparation:

1. First peel the kiwis, oranges and bananas. Cut the kiwis into slices and halve them, divide the oranges into wedges and halve the bananas lengthwise.
2. On a large plate, make the bottom of the island out of the orange wedges. The banana halves are the palm tree trunks, the kiwi slices are the palm tree leaves and the blueberries are the coconuts.
3. Finally, drizzle a little lemon juice over the banana halves to prevent them from turning brown.

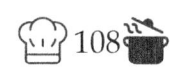

# Greek Style Yoghurt

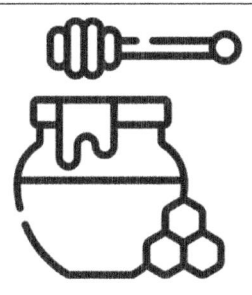

### Ingredients for 4 servings:
**Preparation time: approx. 5 minutes**

- 600 g Greek-style yoghurt (4x150 g cups)
- 4 tablespoons honey
- To garnish: Fruit to taste (e.g. strawberries), coconut flakes

### Preparation:

1. Divide the yoghurt into four bowls.
2. Pour one tablespoon of honey per bowl over the yoghurt.
3. Before serving, garnish with strawberries and coconut flakes, for example.

# Vegan Chocolate Porridge

### Ingredients for 2 servings:

- 90 grams tender oat flakes
- 300 ml hazelnut milk/almond milk
- 1 tbsp maple syrup
- A pinch of cinnamon
- 1 tbsp cocoa powder
- Topping:
- One banana and 1 tbsp chopped nuts

### Preparation:

1. Take a pot and mix the oat flakes, cocoa, cinnamon, maple syrup and milk together. Bring everything to the boil and then take the pot off the cooker to let the mixture swell for about 10 minutes, covered.
2. Now the finished porridge can be divided into two portions and put into bowls. Finally, add the sliced banana and the chopped nuts as a topping to the porridge. Enjoy it now!

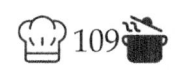

# Waffles with Coconut

### Ingredients:
(approx. 6 waffles)

- 65 grams soft, dried apricots
- 100 ml oat milk
- 180 grams spelt flour
- 1 tsp baking powder
- 200 g coconut milk
- 50 grams coconut oil

### Preparation:

1. Put the apricots, coconut milk, coconut oil and oat milk in a pot and heat everything for about 6 minutes.
2. Puree everything with a hand blender or stand mixer.
3. Now add the coconut flakes, flour and baking powder to the pureed ingredients. Now pour the finished batter into a waffle iron.

# Fruit Bar

### Ingredients:

- 75 ml pure fruit juice (apple, grape, orange, etc.)
- 100 g oat flakes/ almond flour/ cornflakes
- Optional: 40 grams nuts
- Baking wafers
- 250 g unsulphured dried fruit of your choice

### Preparation:

1. Put all the above ingredients in a blender and puree everything to a fine paste.
2. Take two wafers for each fruit bar and spread one half with the fruit mixture. Then fold the other half on top.
3. Then place the finished fruit bars on a board and another board on top of the bars so that they stick together nicely without the wafers curling.

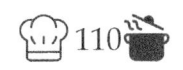

# Apple Pancakes with Wholemeal Flour

### Ingredients:

- 650 ml whole milk
- 125 grams wholemeal flour
- 125 grams wheat flour
- A pinch of salt
- Two eggs
- Optional: a sachet of vanilla powder
- 1 tbsp soft butter
- Two large apples

### Preparation:

1. First, preheat your oven to 200 degrees top and bottom heat.
2. In a bowl, mix the butter, flour, salt, vanilla sugar, eggs and milk together to make a dough.
3. Cut the apples into cubes and mix them into the dough.
4. Put the dough into a higher baking tray covered with baking paper. Now the dough can go into the oven for 25 minutes.
5. Serve the pancakes with some fruit or fruit puree.

**NOTES**

# ONE POT
## VEGETARIAN & MORE

### ICE CREAM

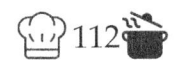

# Banana Ice Cream

### Ingredients:

- one large and ripe banana
- three ice sticks

### Preparation:

1. Cut the peeled banana into three pieces.
2. Now skewer the three pieces on the sticks and put the banana skewers in the freezer for about two hours. After that it can be enjoyed.

# Melon Ice Cream

### Ingredients:

- a large watermelon
- Ice cream sticks

### Preparation:

1. Cut the watermelon into thick slices.
2. Now cut the slices into eighths.
3. Now you can cut a slit in the shell with a knife where you can insert the chopstick.
4. Afterwards, all the finished watermelons can be placed in the freezer with the ice cream stick for at least 6 hours.

# Avocado Ice Cream

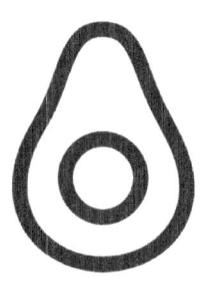

## Ingredients:

- 400 ml coconut milk
- 1 ½ avocado
- Coconut flakes
- 4 tbsp agave syrup
- the juice of one lime

## Preparation:

1. Beat the creamy coconut milk mixture with a hand mixer until creamy.
2. Now halve the avocados, remove the pit so that you can easily take out the flesh and put it in a bowl.
3. Gradually pour the lime juice over the avocados and mix together until creamy.
4. Now fold the avocado with the lime and the agave syrup or another sweetener of your choice into the whipped coconut milk.
5. Now put the finished ice cream mixture into a smaller bowl or baking dish and cover it with cling film. After about 5 hours in the freezer, the mixture should have become a delicious ice cream.

# Mango-Pineapple-Coconut Ice Cream

### Ingredients:
- 150 ml coconut milk
- 1 tbsp maple syrup
- 80 grams mango
- 80 grams pineapple
- Half a banana
- A pinch of vanilla
- A dash of lemon juice

### Preparation:
1. Puree the peeled and chopped mango, banana and pineapple with a blender or in a blender.
2. Add the creamy coconut milk, maple syrup, vanilla and dash of lemon juice to the pureed mixture and mix together.
3. Now the ice cream mixture can be filled into ice cream moulds and placed in the freezer for about three hours.

# Raspberry Banana Ice Cream

### Ingredients:
(four servings)

- 300 g frozen raspberries
- Three bananas
- Half a litre of water

### Preparation:
1. Cut the bananas into small pieces and mash them with the raspberries and the water, which you should add little by little so that the mixture does not become too liquid.
2. Now everything can be placed in the freezer for a few hours. Meanwhile, it is good to stir the mixture several times.

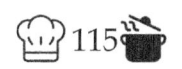

# Strawberry Yoghurt Ice Cream

### Ingredients:

- 150 grams yoghurt
- 200 grams strawberries
- Half a banana
- A pinch of vanilla
- 1 tsp maple syrup

### Preparation:

1. Cut the washed strawberries into quarters. Then put them in a blender or puree them with a hand blender.
2. Then mix in the yoghurt, maple syrup and vanilla.
3. Finally, the ice cream moulds can be filled with the finished ice cream mixture and placed in the freezer for about three hours.

# Fruit Lollipop

### Ingredients:

- Any fruit, e.g. kiwi, melon, mango
- Short skewers/straws

### Preparation:

1. Cut the fruit of your choice into 1 cm pieces.
2. Then skewer the cut fruit on a short skewer, which should not be pointed, or on a short straw.
3. The skewers can now already be enjoyed or you can put them in the freezer for a few more hours.

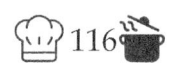

# Apricot and Coconut Ice Cream

### Ingredients:

- 700 grams apricots
- 150 grams yoghurt
- 6 tbsp coconut flakes

### Preparation:

1. Remove all the seeds from the apricots and then cut them into pieces.
2. Mix the apricots with the coconut flakes and the yoghurt using a blender.
3. Now put the ice cream in the freezer for about three hours. Again, the mixture should be stirred several times.

# Berry Ice Cream

### Ingredients:

- 250 grams frozen berries
- 300 grams yoghurt
- 1 tbsp maple syrup

### Preparation:

1. Puree the berries after you have let them thaw a little.
2. Then add the yoghurt and maple syrup and mix everything together well.
3. Pour the mixture into a suitable bowl and place it in the freezer for at least three hours. Again, stir the ice cream several times.

# Raspberry-Mango Ice Cream

## Ingredients:

(for 6 ice cream moulds)
- One ripe mango
- 50 grams raspberries
- Ice moulds
- Approx. 200 g Greek yoghurt (10% fat)

## Preparation:

1. Peel the mango and then cut off the flesh. Put the pulp in a blender with the raspberries and puree.
2. Now mix the fruit pulp with the Greek yoghurt. Now you can fill both together into ice cream moulds and put them in the freezer for several hours. After that, the delicious ice cream can be served and enjoyed.

# Yoghurt Ice Cream Vanilla Mango

## Ingredients:

- ½ very ripe mango
- some vanilla pulp
- 125 g natural yoghurt (10% fat)

## Preparation:

1. Put the yoghurt in a bowl and mix it with the vanilla.
2. Then peel the mango and cut it into small pieces, which you then puree with a blender.
3. First fill the mango puree into the ice cream moulds and then the yoghurt on top. Place the ice cream moulds in the freezer for about 6 hours until the ice cream is firm.

## Strawberry Ice Cream

**Ingredients:**
**(2 servings)**

- 50 g coconut yoghurt/natural yoghurt
- 200 g frozen strawberries
- One ripe banana
- Ice moulds

**Preparation:**

1. Fill the already defrosted strawberries into a blender and then add the chopped banana. Now add the yoghurt and mix everything together.
2. Fill the mixture into the ice cream moulds and put them in the freezer for about 2 hours. The ice cream is ready!

## Frozen Yoghurt

**Ingredients:**
**(for 6 ice cream moulds)**

- 3- 4 ripe apricots
- 120 grams Greek yoghurt (10% fat)
- Ice moulds

**Preparation:**

1. Put the apricots and yoghurt in a blender and puree. Now pour the mixture into the ice cream moulds and place them in the freezer for 12 hours.

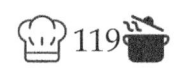

# Kiwi Popsicle

### Ingredients:
(for 8 ice cream moulds)

- 7 Kiwis
- 1 lime
- Popsicle moulds with handle

### Preparation:

1. Clean & peel the kiwis. Cut one kiwi into very thin slices. Squeeze the lime well.
2. Puree the remaining kiwi with the lime juice.
3. Place the kiwi slices in ice-cream moulds. Pour the fruit puree into the moulds and place in the freezer for 40 minutes. Then place popsicle sticks in the centre of the ice cream. Leave the ice cream to freeze for at least 3 hours.

# Capri Ice Cream a la Casa

### Ingredients:
(for 6 ice cream moulds)

- 600 ml orange juice
- 1/2 lime
- Popsicle moulds with handle

### Preparation:

1. Squeeze the lime well and mix with the orange juice.
2. Put everything into the ice-cream moulds and put them in the freezer over night.

# ONE POT
## VEGETARIAN & MORE

## DRINKS

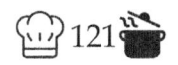

# Herbal Ginger Spice Tea

## Ingredients for 4 glasses:

- 80 g ginger
- 1 bunch sage
- 2 sprigs rosemary
- 1 organic lemon
- 2 Star anise
- 1 cinnamon stick

### Preparation:

1. Peel the ginger and cut into thin slices, wash the sage and rosemary thoroughly, wash the lemon with hot water, halve it and cut off three thin slices.
2. Put the ginger, herbs, star anise, cinnamon stick and lemon in a teapot. Fill with 1 litre of boiling hot water. Let everything steep for 6-8 minutes, then strain and sip. Can be enjoyed hot or cold.

# Infused Water

## Ingredients for 8 glasses:

- 50 g ginger
- 200 g organic cucumber
- 1 organic orange
- 1 pomegranate
- 1 bunch mint
- 2 L mineral water

### Preparation:

1. Wash the ingredients and peel if necessary. Slice the ginger, cucumber and 'orange. Remove the pomegranate seeds. Pluck the mint. Put everything in a carafe, fill with mineral water and chill for 2 hours.

# Pineapple-Lime Drink

## Ingredients for 4 glasses:

- 500 g pineapple
- 1 Apple
- 2 organic limes
- 125 g organic raspberries, frozen
- 500 ml mineral water

### Preparation:

1. Peel the pineapple, remove the stalk and cut into small pieces. Wash and quarter the apple. Then remove the core and cut the apple quarters into pieces.
2. Wash the limes under running hot water, finely puree the pineapple and apple cubes together with the water using a blender. Add the juice of one lime and fill into glasses together with some ice cubes.
3. Cut the second lime into thin slices and garnish the glasses with them. Lightly press on the frozen raspberries and place them on top.

# Lemon Ginger Lemonade

## Ingredients for 4 glasses:

- 1 litre mineral water
- 3 tbsp ginger juice
- 2 lemons
- 15 ice cubes

### Preparation:

1. Pour the mineral water into a large carafe and add the ginger juice.
2. Squeeze the lemons and stir in the juice.
3. Add ice cubes and enjoy.

# Peach Iced Tea

### Ingredients for 4 glasses:

- 1 litre water
- 3 bags rooibos tea
- 4 peaches
- 15 ice cubes

### Preparation:

1. Cut three of the four peaches into small pieces.
2. Pour boiling water into the tea bag and add the peach pieces. Let the tea steep according to the instructions.
3. Remove the tea bags after the specified time and leave the rest in the fridge with half the ice cubes for a good 1 hour.
4. Then remove the peach pieces again and fill up with the remaining ice cubes. Cut the last peach freshly into wedges and divide among the glasses.
5. If necessary, sweeten with peach juice and decorate with mint or lemon balm.

# Pomegranate Lemonade

### Ingredients for 4 glasses:

- 1 pomegranate
- 1 lemon
- 1 litre
- 2 sprigs mint
- 8 ice cubes

### Preparation:

1. Cut the pomegranate in half and juice each half with a lemon squeezer. Then squeeze the lemon.
2. In a jug, mix the pomegranate juice with the juice of the lemon. Also add a few pomegranate seeds.
3. Add a litre of mineral water and serve with 2 ice cubes per glass and a few mint leaves.

# Cucumber Mint Lemonade

### Ingredients for 4 glasses:

- 1 bunch mint
- 1 medium organic lemon
- 1/2 medium cucumber
- 1000 ml water
- 8 ice cubes

### Preparation:

1. Wash the mint.
2. Wash the cucumber and lemon thoroughly and cut into slices.
3. Mix the cucumber and lemon slices with about 4 mint stalks and the water in a carafe. Leave to infuse.
4. Fill glasses each with 2 ice cubes and 1 stem of mint and top up with the cucumber lemonade, fish a few slices of cucumber from the carafe and add.

# Strawberry and Rosehip Iced Tea

### Ingredients for 4 glasses:

- 1000 ml water
- 3 bags rose hip tea
- 1 medium lime(s)
- 100 g strawberry(s)
- 15 ice cubes

### Preparation:

1. Boil the rosehip tea according to the instructions and then leave to cool.
2. Pour the tea into a jug with half the ice cubes and place in the fridge for a good 1 hour.
3. Squeeze the lime and add the juice.
4. Slice the strawberries and the other half of the lime and add to the tea with the remaining ice cubes.

# Orange-Lemon Iced Tea

### Ingredients for 4 glasses:

- 1000 ml water
- 3 green tea bags
- 16 ice cubes
- 1 medium orange(s) (organic)
- 1 medium lemon(s) (organic)
- 1/2 medium lime(s)

### Preparation:

1. Prepare the tea according to the instructions. Then remove the tea bags and allow the tea to cool.
2. Put the tea in a jug with half the ice cubes and chill in the fridge for about an hour.
3. In the meantime, cut the orange and lemon into thin slices. Squeeze the lime.
4. After the tea has become refreshingly cold in the refrigerator, add the orange and lemon and refine with the juice of the lime. Serve the iced tea with 2 ice cubes per glass.

**NOTES**

_____

_____

_____

_____

_____

_____

_____

# Closing words

Thank you so much for choosing my book.

I hope you got some ideas and inspiration.

I hope you enjoy cooking more and would be very happy if you recommend this book to your friends, family and loved ones. Feel free to leave me feedback via a review.

Yours, Clara de Vries

I'm also on Instagram and post inspiring food pictures every day.

You can find me at        clara_en_food

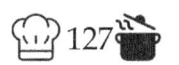

**Clara De Vries**

# Legal

## Imprint

1st edition 2021

Clara de Vries is represented by:

Contact: Daniel Schneider/ Vollersdorfer Str. 56 A/ 07548 Gera

All rights reserved.

Reproduction in whole or in part is prohibited.

No part of this work may be reproduced, duplicated or distributed in any form without the written permission of the author.

## Liability for external links

The book contains links to external websites of third parties over whose content the author has no influence. Therefore, no liability can be assumed for the content of external websites. The respective provider or operator of the website is responsible for the content of the linked websites. The linked pages were checked for possible legal violations at the time of linking. Illegal contents were not recognisable at the time of linking. However, a permanent control of the contents of the linked websites is not reasonable without concrete indications of an infringement. Such links will be removed immediately if infringements of the law become known.